Meeting God

# Meeting
# God

Peter Jeffery

EVANGELICAL PRESS

EVANGELICAL PRESS
Faverdale North, Darlington, DL3 0PH, England

e-mail: sales@evangelicalpress.org

Evangelical Press USA
P. O. Box 825, Webster, New York 14580, USA

e-mail: usa.sales@evangelicalpress.org

web: http://www.evangelicalpress.org

First published 2008

**British Library Cataloguing in Publication Data available**

ISBN-13  978-0-85234-671-6          ISBN 0-85234-671-9

Unless otherwise indicated, Scripture quotations are taken from the Holy Bible, New International Version. Copyright © 1973, 1978, 1984 by International Bible Society. Used by permission of Hodder & Stoughton, a division of Hodder Headline Ltd. All rights reserved. 'NIV' is a registered trademark of International Bible Society. UK trademark number 1448790.

Printed and bound in Great Britain by Biddles Ltd, King's Lynn, Norfolk, UK.

# Contents

# Introduction

In this book you will see people having dealings with God. Some met God, but sadly others did not. The vital question is: do you want to meet God and if so, how can this be done?

The following chapters seek to help you in this. From simple illustrations and the lives of a selection of individuals from the Bible you will see that you need Jesus to be your Saviour, as he is the way God has prescribed for sinners to meet with him.

# 1.
# Terror in the city

Whenever evil rears its ugly head with such devastating effect as it did in New York and Washington on September 11, 2001, people almost inevitably ask, 'Why doesn't God do something about it?'

We recognize the evil, and the question implies that God ought to deal with it; but do we understand that we are part of the evil? Evil is always a matter of degree. An IRA bomb planted in an English city and killing a few innocent people is only a matter of degree from flying an airliner into the World Trade Centre and killing thousands. It is the same evil in the human heart that propagates both actions.

Evil has to be seen as a matter of terrorism against God because Jesus said that the problem is that men love evil and this produces a heart that rebels against God and rejects his authority. Thus man is capable of any atrocity — terrorism, murder, adultery, pride, envy, gossip — all stem from a rejection of God's way.

The Bible calls it sin, and God *has* done something about it.

Whether a man calls himself a Christian, or a Muslim, or an atheist — all of us are sinners by nature and action. It is in order to deal with this sin that God sent Jesus into the world. Are we so eager for God to deal with our sin and evil?

Because there is sin in our hearts, we deliberately go against what God says we should do, wanting our way rather than his. Indeed, our whole lives consist of rebellion against God. Sin is part of our very nature.

There are people today foolish enough to think that sin does not matter. We should 'live and let live', they say. So sin is made the focus of entertainment: it is played with, applauded and generally looked upon as harmless. Then it explodes in our faces as it did on September 11, and we are shocked. But the shock only shows that we have never understood its full implications.

Sin is like a cancer. Terrorism is only one of its more extreme symptoms. Sin is seen first in its disregard for God, and then spreads to a lack of concern for others. It emerges in the selfishness and greed of ordinary people and in the breakdown of family life. By our sin we all contribute to the mess the world is in, and we all suffer because of it. But there is even worse news. God holds us accountable for the way we live our lives. He does not turn a blind eye to our sin. Our sin and rebellion against God have created an unbridgeable gap between ourselves and God. The Bible says that spiritually we are 'dead' because of our sin. We can do nothing to bridge the gap, but we would be foolish to ignore the problem.

# 2.

# Noah

Every good thing Noah did was in response to either a command or action of God, and it is impossible to understand Noah apart from his relationship with God.

We know of this man because of his ark. But really it wasn't his ark at all; it was God's ark. It was God's holiness that made it necessary and it was God's grace that provided it. Noah was only the contractor employed by God to build it.

Why was the ark necessary?

We read in Genesis 6:5-7: 'The LORD saw how great man's wickedness on the earth had become, and that every inclination of the thoughts of his heart was only evil all the time. The LORD was grieved that he had made man on the earth, and his heart was filled with pain. So the LORD said, "I will wipe mankind, whom I have created, from the face of the earth — men and animals, and creatures that move along the ground, and birds of the air — for I am grieved that I have made them."'

So it was human sin and God's reaction to it that made the ark necessary. God is holy and human sin not only grieves his heart but also fills it with pain. It is not that God is a 'killjoy' and does not like to see men enjoying themselves. Nor is it that God is too sensitive and ought to give and take a little. God is holy and our sin is an attack upon that holiness.

Sometimes sin is violent and evil, sometimes it is pleasant and attractive; but always it is opposed to God and always God is opposed to it. God's wrath is an inevitable product of his holiness. The Flood was the evidence of the awful wrath of God but it was also the evidence that the God we have to deal with is a holy God. It was human sin and divine holiness that made the ark necessary. Without it mankind had no hope.

## Why was the ark built?

It was not Noah's idea. It was God who decided it would be built and God who designed it.

The ark is a vivid symbol of God's grace. It was intended by God as an instrument of deliverance to preserve life on earth. The ark showed that sin would not be ultimately triumphant. God had not finished with sinful men and women but still cared for them in spite of their rebellion.

So on one hand there was man in his sin, and on the other there was God who was about to deal with it. God's first act is one of grace and mercy towards Noah and his family: 'Build an ark,' he says. The ark was huge — one and a half football pitches. It was not until 1858 that a bigger boat was built! It was nothing like the pictures you see in children's books.

Clearly it was too much of a job for only Noah and his sons. He would have had to employ others to do the work — Williams the woodcutter, Jones the joiner, Harris the hammer, Parry the pitch. Many helped build the ark but never got into it, and never were saved. They made a living from the ark but never accepted the God of the ark. They knew all about this boat and could tell you its dimensions and its materials, but they never believed in its purpose. They saw no need for it. They saw no need for salvation because just like people today they saw nothing wrong with their sin and in no way did they take talk of divine judgement seriously.

One of the greatest dangers of sin is that it deludes. Not all sin is the same. Some is more evil and blatant than others. So respectable sinners look down their moral noses at those in their sex, drugs and drunkenness, and say, 'I'm not like that, therefore I'm alright.' But even though all sin is not the same in its outworking, it is all the same in its source. It is all disobedience to the law and word of God. And it is all the same in its consequences — the wage of all sin is death, judgement and hell.

God's second act of grace towards every sinner was that he gave them plenty of time to repent. God was grieved and angry with mankind's sin but even then he gave them 120 years to consider their ways and repent. God always goes beyond what we could expect but that does not change his determination to deal with sin. Will the 120 years make any difference? We can see now that it did not; but the glory of grace is in the Lord who offers it, not in the sinner who may or may not receive it.

How long has God been giving you to repent? How many times have you heard the gospel and still you have not repented? Still you cling to your sin. Still you seek to minimize the seriousness of God's judgement on sin.

## The preacher of righteousness

God's grace to sinners is seen in his willingness to forgive and in his giving the people a preacher to point them on the right way. There would have been no point in giving them 120 years to repent if there was no light of truth shining in the world to point them to God. Faith always comes through hearing God's word (Romans 10:14).

Noah's light shone out in two ways. Firstly, in the act of building the ark. Everyone else was concerned with the here and now. They were 'eating and drinking, marrying and giving in marriage'. Noah also had to eat and drink and obviously he was concerned about marriage because he and his three sons were married. But above all that, he had an eye to the future and to what God had said. His whole life was taken up with the effects of human sin upon the heart of God and God's response to that sin.

By building the ark he showed the unbelieving world that he took God seriously. Every plank he sawed, every nail he hammered told the world that God was holy and would not tolerate their sin. The only reason for the ark was the reality of human sin and the fact that God was going to deal with it.

Do you take God seriously? Do you think that sin makes no difference? Do you believe the 'fairy story' or rather the devil's story, that God will not condemn anyone to hell and in the end we will all go to heaven? It's a lie that has no substance in the New Testament.

Sin is horrendous. Your sin is grieving God and he has stated very clearly in the Bible what the outcome of that will be.

To these people God sent a preacher. Now to the thinking of many this would be wholly irrelevant. What use is a preacher? But this was God's way, and it still is. The history of our country alone is testimony to the fact that when this land has sunk as spiritually and morally low as the people of Noah's day, God has brought it back to sanity and truth by sending preachers to preach the gospel in the power of the Holy Spirit.

It is interesting to see how the New Testament describes the preaching of Noah. 2 Peter 2:5 says he was a preacher of righteousness. Notice that it does not say 'a preacher of judgement'. He must have told them of the coming judgement and of the flood, but his emphasis was not on this but on righteousness: the righteousness that God demands and which they had failed to meet; and righteousness as God's requirement for salvation.

Basically, his message was no different from that of Paul in the New Testament. In the opening chapter of Romans, Paul tells us why the gospel is so important: 'I am not ashamed of the gospel, because it is the power of God for the salvation of everyone who believes… For in the gospel a righteousness from God is revealed, a righteousness that is by faith' (v. 16).

Righteousness means conforming to God's standards. It is what is acceptable to God. So righteousness in man means that he is capable of meeting God's standards. This being the case, man's greatest need is to be righteous, to be acceptable to God. But 'there is none righteous', says Romans 3. So the prime function of the gospel is to provide for the guilty sinner what he most needs. This righteousness comes to us through faith in Jesus Christ (Romans 3:21-22).

The people of Noah's time, whose every inclination and thought was only evil all the time, did not need religion or moral exhortation. They needed to find what Noah found — grace in the eyes of the Lord. They needed something done *to* them and *for* them, for which there was no other explanation than the fact that God had done it.

This is exactly what we need today. Nothing else will deal with our sin to the satisfaction of God. If we are to be saved, God must do it. For the people of Noah's day the ark was God's means to this glorious end.

## How did sinners respond to the offer of God's mercy?

They would have responded in exactly the same way as people do today. Some had spent their whole life helping Noah build the ark, as had their fathers before them. They felt an attachment to the construction. They could say, 'I remember my father putting that section together.' They had no idea or sympathy as to the purpose of the ark but certainly there was an affection for it.

Today people may say, 'My grandfather helped build this church. I was brought along as a babe in arms. It's my church. I love every brick and pew.' But what about the gospel? What about Jesus?

Others would agree with Noah denouncing sin, but would say, 'Don't you think you're a bit too narrow? There is no harm in our sin. We are not sinners. Denounce the world but not us.'

Others liked old Noah and said, 'We don't mind coming into your ark but we are not too keen on your God.' But you cannot have the ark without God. You cannot have salvation without the God of salvation.

Others perhaps would have liked a job building the ark and would show an interest, but their eye was on what they could get out of it, not on their need of what the ark offered as a means of salvation.

Most would have thought it all a joke. They regarded any talk of rain as nonsense. Who could be expected to take Noah seriously? He was a crank. When the rain began to fall, some who perhaps were more discerning than the rest thought there may be something in what Noah said: 'We'll be on the safe side and have the ark just in case, but we don't really want God.'

It's not a lot different today, is it? Are you like these people? Be warned. God told Noah and his family to go into the ark and then he shut them in. God closed the door. The offer of salvation was no longer available. The day of grace was over. The rain fell and the waters rose. People now believed all that Noah had preached — but it was too late. They would cry out for Noah to let them in, but Noah had no control over the door. God had shut it.

Listen to the words of Jesus in Matthew 24:37-42: 'As it was in the days of Noah, so it will be at the coming of the Son of Man. For in the days before the flood, people were eating and drinking, marrying and giving in marriage, up to the day Noah entered the ark; and they knew nothing about what would happen until the flood came and took them all away. That is how it will be at the coming of the Son of Man. Two men will be in the field; one will be taken and the other left. Two women will be grinding with a hand mill; one will be taken and the other left. Therefore keep watch, because you do not know on what day your Lord will come.'

The ark was the provision of God's love and mercy and is an illustration of what the cross is. God will deal with sin once and for all; there is no doubt of that. We are all sinners therefore we all need a place of safety when that judgement falls. This is what the cross of Jesus offers us. The door, the way to Christ and salvation, is still open; but if you want salvation you had better seek it now because the day of grace will not always be with us. This is urgent.

Jesus said, 'I am the door. I am the way.' On the cross he took the judgement of God that your sin deserved. He paid the debt that you owed for breaking the law of God. He did all this because he loves you and does not want you to go to hell. Come to him now.

# 3.

# The heart of man

The specialist in hospital told me that my heart was in a serious condition. How did he know? First of all, he was guided by the symptoms — pain, tightening of the chest, breathlessness and an inability to do ordinary things. There is a great deal of heart trouble today and many will recognize these symptoms, although thankfully most people do not suffer in this way.

Yet God says that we *all* have a serious heart condition, and in the Bible he spells out the symptoms:

'The heart is deceitful above all things and beyond cure. Who can understand it?'

(Jeremiah 17:9).

'For out of the heart come evil thoughts, murder, adultery, sexual immorality, theft, false testimony, slander. These are what make a man "unclean"'

(Matthew 15:19-20).

Our sins are the evidence of our heart condition. Sin always brings *pain*; it appears to be enjoyable but always ends in unhappiness. Sin brings *breathlessness*, an absence of the life-giving breath of the Holy Spirit. Sin renders us *unable to do* the things we were created for — to love and serve God.

## Do you have these symptoms?

If you were told by a heart specialist that you had a serious heart condition, you would be a fool to ignore it. What is your reaction to God's diagnosis of your heart? Do you take it seriously? Are you anxious for a cure?

Having considered the symptoms, the doctor then examined my heart more closely. A painless and fascinating technique enabled him to show me my own heart on a TV screen and point out to me what was wrong and what needed to be done.

God shows us our heart. He knows the exact condition it is in. Often we may look reasonably healthy on the surface; morally and socially we may be very acceptable. But how does *God* see us?

In the Bible God often refers to the heart of man. There we read that the apostle Peter told a respectable man that in God's sight his heart was not right. The same is true of us all.

What causes heart trouble?

The heart specialist will cite things like cigarettes, wrong diet and lack of exercise as the main culprits for causing physical heart trouble. Spiritually, our heart problems are caused by *sin*; that is, a rejection of God's ways.

What is the remedy?

The consultant told me that the only answer was *surgery*. My problem was a blockage of the arteries. This had to be dealt with to allow the blood to do its job of taking oxygen to my heart. Therefore, I needed a bypass operation.

This involves the surgeon taking a vein from the leg and using it to bypass the blockage in the artery, thus allowing a full flow of life-giving blood. This was the only answer to my heart problem.

In the same way, the only answer to the *spiritual* need of all our hearts is for the blood of Jesus Christ to do its work of bringing forgiveness and life. What Jesus did for us on the cross is the *only* thing that can make sinners clean in God's sight.

Our problem is *sin*. It pollutes the heart and makes us unacceptable to God. *But Jesus came into the world to deal with sin.*

He did this once and for all on the cross, by taking the punishment our sins deserved. *He died in our place.* That is why the Bible speaks of salvation through his blood. Morality, religion and education are no remedy for our heart condition. The only answer acceptable to God is *Jesus*.

The greatest heart specialist, God himself, has diagnosed the condition of your heart.

It is serious.

It is fatal.

It is terminal.

*You need a new heart.*

God does not do bypass operations; his surgery is much more radical.

According to the Bible he takes away the stony heart — the one that is blocked, hard and unresponsive to God — and gives a new one! God will give this to *you* when you turn away from your sin and trust with your whole being in the Lord Jesus.

# 4.

# Lot

If you read the story of Lot in Genesis 19 you would come to the conclusion that he was a wicked sinful man. He was typical of the man of the world and apart from his relationship to Abraham there seems nothing to commend him. But according to 2 Peter 2:7-8 he was a righteous man. That means he was acceptable to God.

We have to ask, on what terms? The biblical answer has to be that it was on the same terms as Abraham: 'Abraham believed the Lord, and he credited it to him as righteousness' (Genesis 15:6). The New Testament says that Abraham was justified by faith (Romans 4). Peter said the same thing was true of Lot and he gives evidence to support his claim by declaring that Lot was 'tormented in his righteous soul by the lawless deeds he saw and heard' (2 Peter 2:8).

Lot was, in New Testament terms, a Christian, but he was a very weak man. He lived in days when to love and serve God was rare. Sodom, the city he lived in, had a reputation for evil: 'Then the Lord said, "The outcry against Sodom and Gomorrah is so great and their sin so grievous that I will go down and see if what they have done is as bad as the outcry that has reached me'" (Genesis 18:20-21). Their great sin was sexual perversion, hence the term 'sodomite' refers to a homosexual. This sin was rampant right throughout the city. You may remember the amazing dialogue when Abraham pleads with God to spare Sodom. Not even ten good men could be found in the city (Genesis 18). It was in this environment that Lot lived. A man of faith as strong as Abraham would have had difficulty living in Sodom; to a weak character like Lot, it was impossible.

The Christian always has problems in this world. There are some times in history when it is easier to be a Christian than at other times. For instance, one hundred years ago it was fairly normal to attend church. Not so now. Today Christians are regarded as 'odd-bods', old-fashioned, or a left-over from a previous century. So it is not easy to be a believer, especially a keen and committed one. You may well be dismissed as an extreme fundamentalist. In such a situation it is easy to compromise and water down your beliefs to make them more acceptable to the world. We all know something of this temptation. Lot certainly did and sadly he gave in to it. He was a weak man with more than one foot in the world.

## Why was he in Sodom?

As we see from Genesis 13, Lot was in Sodom out of his own choice. He was Abraham's nephew and clearly this is where he learnt about God. He saw the example of his uncle and listened to his words. And he prospered while he was with Abraham. But this is where his problem began.

This prosperity made it necessary for him to leave the godly influence of his uncle. Lot was given the choice of where he was to go, but his choice was made for wrong motives: 'Lot looked up and saw that the whole plain of the Jordan was well watered, like the garden of the LORD… So Lot chose for himself the whole plain of the Jordan and set out towards the east' (Genesis 13:10-11).

He was thinking only in terms of ease and wealth, and completely ignored the spiritual consequences: 'Lot lived among the cities of the plain and pitched his tents near Sodom. Now the men of Sodom were wicked and were sinning greatly against the LORD' (vv. 12-13).

The application is very clear for us because so many Christians make the same mistake. A promotion at work means moving home and leaving a good biblical church. The decision is taken simply on material grounds and very often is spiritually disastrous as the new home has no good church in the area.

Lot's choice did not come from a deliberate action of sin. He did not choose to be like the people of Sodom. His failure came because he did not act on biblical principles.

He first of all pitched his tents *near* Sodom, but soon he was living in that evil place. The righteous man is in a most unrighteous place. And he was not there as a missionary or evangelist. He was not there out of concern for lost souls, but out of personal ambition and greed.

He was in a place of no fellowship with no Abraham to instruct him, and a place where his family comes under the evil influence of Sodom. The vileness of his daughter's actions in 19:30-38 can be traced to the sexual perversion of Sodom they had grown up in. Lot may have hated the sin of the city, but his daughters loved it and so too did his wife. A Christian father has a great responsibility in where he takes his family to live and therefore it is a decision that should be taken prayerfully with an eye on God's will, not material prosperity.

## Why did Lot not leave Sodom?

Was it because his business was doing too well? Was it because his family were happy there and he was too weak to give a lead? Lot was certainly a weak man and one who dithered. Even when the angel was leading him out of Sodom he hesitated. How weak most of us are before the pulls and attractions of the world! All too often we hesitate when we should act. We look, instead of rushing away.

The only consolation here is the vivid reminder that salvation is all of grace. Here was a righteous man, but what a mess he was making of everything. Nothing but grace could have saved Lot. If left to himself, he would still have been in Sodom when God destroyed it.

Moral weakness, greed and sloth are deadly charac-teristics to see in a Christian. We may delight in salvation by grace, but at the same time our lives may be damning others. If sin can have this effect upon a righteous man, what can it do to an unrighteous man? It will dominate, twist, control and then destroy.

## Genesis 19

Genesis 19 is a remarkable chapter. We see the depravity of men and women in sin and we see how blatant sin can be. We see also that God will always deal with sin. Above all, we see the amazing love and grace of God in redeeming one of his people.

In chapter 18 Abraham has three visitors — angels. Two of these go on to Sodom to see Lot who greets them warmly and with hospitality. As far as he understands things they are men not angels. In 19:1-3 we see something of grace in Lot's life. He is polite, courteous and hospitable. Then in verse 4 things begin to get nasty.

The men of Sodom had heard about Lot's visitors and came looking to have sex with them. Another glimpse of grace is seen in Lot as he pleads with the Sodomites, 'Don't do this wicked thing.' This is encouraging, but what then do we make of Lot offering those evil men his two daughters so that 'you can do what you like with them'. He seeks to remedy sin with more sin. It is only the intervention of the Lord that saves the situation as the angels strike the crowd of men blind.

It seems as if this is the last straw and the Lord decides to destroy Sodom. Lot is warned of what is going to happen and urged to get his family out of the city. When he tells his two sons-in-law of the coming judgement they think he is joking. Why is this? Is it because they think that any idea of judgement is nonsense? Is it because they see nothing wrong with homosexuality? Is it because the warning comes from Lot, who up to this point had shown no serious spiritual inclinations?

The angels urge speed upon Lot, but he hesitates. Then he whimpers that he will not be able to reach safety. How patient God has to be with us! It is easy to criticize Lot but there is too much of him in all of us. The lessons from the life of this man are clear.

To the non-Christian, Lot says, 'Get right with God.' Take sin seriously. Today homosexuality is as acceptable almost as it was in Sodom; but not with God. But this is only one sin, and all sin — homosexuality, pride, envy, gossip etc. — is under the divine pronouncement of judgement. We all need a righteousness to make us acceptable to God; but how do we get it? We cannot buy it or earn it, but like Abraham and Lot it can be credited to us, as we shall see in later chapters.

To the Christian, the life of Lot challenges us to what sort of Christian life we are living. Your credited righteousness will get you to heaven but will your lifestyle prevent others getting there? And perhaps more importantly, will it prevent your family getting there?

The story of Lot and Sodom is one of judgement but clearly in it all can be seen the wonder of the grace and mercy of God. We are told in verse 16 that the Lord was merciful to them.

Cannot every believer say that about themselves? We no more deserve mercy than Lot's family, but thank you, Lord, for such grace. How much sin is in our lives! How often we grieve and dishonour God! We are not to trade on the grace of God. Praise him for grace — o yes; but do not take it for granted.

# 5.

# The missed flight

I have flown across the Atlantic about thirty times and never had any serious problem until the flight from Los Angeles to London in September 2000. I was travelling with my wife and two friends, and we arrived at Los Angeles International Airport in plenty of time for the 7.30 evening flight to Heathrow. We walked up to the check-in desk with no concerns — we had the tickets, we were in time, so what could go wrong? This was to turn out to be a very false optimism.

The United Airlines official was very polite, but she said, 'I am sorry, sir, but these tickets are not valid for this flight.' I looked at her in amazement. Of course they were valid. She must be making a mistake. She then pointed out to me that the departure time on my tickets was 12.35 not 7.30. I was shocked. I am not stupid. I could not have made a mistake like that. But I had made a very serious mistake. The flight we were booked on had gone several hours earlier.

I am normally very organized and usually check details several times. How could I have made a mistake like that?

The time of departure was very clear on the ticket, and, later, when I looked in my diary, I had written 12.35 as the time to leave. So why had I got it into my head that we were due to leave at 7.30pm? Why did I not look at the tickets? Why did I assume I knew the correct time when clearly I did not?

United Airlines did what they could, but the 7.30pm flight was fully booked. All they could do was to put us on stand-by. This meant we could only have seats if someone else did not turn up. Stand-by gives you no guarantees and you do not know until just before take-off if they have room for you. The stress of that situation was not to my liking at all. Fortunately there was room, and eventually we got home.

## Check the details

The whole sorry episode reminds us how vital it is that when an important journey is coming up, we should assume nothing and check all the details.

The most important of all journeys awaits every one of us. There is a trip from life via death to God and eternity that everyone must take. Jesus said that for that journey there will be many who will 'check-in' very confident that everything is all right. They will come boldly to the Lord. They will speak enthusiastically of all their qualifications to be accepted by God, only to be told there is no room for them. What they assume to be enough to get them to heaven is totally inadequate.

Will you be like that? Are you one of those who assume you will be acceptable to God? Do you think you have done enough to get to heaven? If so, then check the details.

## The details

God says that no one who has sinned in any way will get to heaven, and the Bible makes it very clear that we have *all* sinned. The gospel offers us forgiveness of sins through what Jesus did for us on the cross. It offers us a new start, but we must be born again.

- *Do you consider these to be irrelevant details?*

- *Do you think that being saved and being born again do not apply to you?*

- *Do you know better than God does?*

- *Are you assuming that you will be all right as long as you have tried your best?*

After all, God cannot expect more than that. But he *does* expect more than that. God expects that you conform to his standards, and all misguided assumption, no matter how genuine, will not be accepted.


## Clear

My ticket was clear enough, I just ignored it. God's requirements for heaven are much clearer, and we dare not ignore them. If we do, there is no second chance. There are no stand-by seats for heaven. You must have a booked seat, fully paid for and reserved in your name.

Jesus is the only one who can make us acceptable to God. Forget your assumptions. They are worthless. Trust only in what God has done for you in and through his Son, the Lord Jesus Christ. When Jesus takes care of getting you to heaven there are no mistakes. There are no unforeseen problems. There is no possibility of you missing the 'flight'.

# 6.
# Lot's wife

In chapter four we looked at the story of Lot and now we turn our attention to his wife. The Bible does not have a great deal to say about this woman, but what is said is important enough for Jesus to tell us to remember her (Luke 17:32).

In Luke 17 Jesus had been talking about his Second Coming and the final judgement. Noah and Lot are used by Jesus as examples because the judgement they faced was terrible. In Noah's time it was the Flood and in Lot's day the destruction of Sodom. These events were terrible and absolute. We read that God 'destroyed them all'. What led up to these awful demonstrations of divine justice will be repeated again in the days leading up to Christ's Second Coming: 'Just as it was in the days of Noah, so also will it be in the days of the Son of Man' (v. 26).

We can read of these events in the Old Testament, but how real are they to us? What Jesus is telling us by using them in Luke 17 is that they actually happened. He is not using fairy stories as illustrations of a real event. Both incidents record a judgement on sin that was deserved and total, but it was also a judgement framed in mercy. In each case some were saved even though the vast majority experienced the wrath of God.


## Remember

Why does Jesus draw our attention to this? For the simple reason that it will happen again; and next time it will be final. Most people will say that they do not believe this. On September 10, 2001, most people would have said, 'I don't believe terrorists can hijack airliners and fly them into New York buildings.' But that's exactly what happened on September 11. If evil men can do what many believe is impossible, think what Almighty God can do.

We were all shocked and surprised on September 11, 2001, because it was so unexpected. But the final judgement we have been warned about should not be unexpected because the Bible speaks of it over and over again. The reason for this judgement is sin — and the wages of sin is death. By death, the Bible means three things:

- *Physical death* — the separation of the spirit from the body;
- *Spiritual death* — the separation of the spirit from God;
- *Eternal death* — spiritual death made permanent; in other words, hell.

But even this judgement is framed in mercy because although the wages of sin is death, the gift of God is eternal life (Romans 6:23). God offers sinners pardon in Jesus. The question is: do we take the gift? Jesus knew how few would do this, so he urges us to remember Lot's wife.

The subject of judgement is not pleasant and we are often prone to forget it. Sometimes we do so deliberately, and hide behind thoughts such as, 'God is love so this cannot be true.' Part of this reasoning arises because we forget that God is holy as well as love. God's love and holiness are not in opposition to each other but work together in perfect harmony to fulfil God's will.

## Why Lot's wife?

Why did Jesus single out this woman to bring to our remembrance? In order to answer that question we have to go back to the book of Genesis.

Sodom was an evil city (18:20), and there were not even ten righteous men there (v. 32). Divine judgement was inevitable, yet God in his grace and mercy decided to save Lot and his family (19:15-16). Lot seemed reluctant to be saved and hesitated. He had to be dragged out of Sodom.

God's warning to these reluctant benefactors of his grace was that they were not to look back. Yet Lot's wife did just that, and she was turned into a pillar of salt (19:26). The incident may be strange but the meaning is clear. It was divine judgement, so Jesus says, 'Remember Lot's wife.'

Of all the characters Jesus could have drawn on from the Old Testament, why her? Because she was a woman who had great privileges. In her day, a knowledge of God was rare. There were no Bibles, no churches and no preachers, yet she belonged to a family that God had been especially good to. Compared to millions of others Lot's wife was highly favoured.

She was married to a righteous man and there were not many of those around. It is true that Lot was weak, but he was not evil and blasphemous. She had spent many years living near Abraham. He was righteous and strong. She had seen God rescue her family from captivity by four kings (Genesis 14) with only 318 men.

She would have known of the amazing meeting of Abraham with Melchizedek. She was aware of God's goodness in granting Sarah a son, even though it was physically impossible.

She saw God send two angels to rescue her and her loved ones from coming judgement.

She was amazingly privileged and her life was full of the mercies of God, yet she died in her sin. She died godless and graceless. Her conscience was never challenged and her will was never in submission to God. That is why Jesus said, 'Remember Lot's wife.'

## Our privileges

We have privileges denied to millions. Being born in this country with its history and Christian inheritance we have a wealth of valuable books in the English language, and churches where the gospel is preached. These things are beyond price, but what are we doing with them? Jesus once said to the highly privileged people in the town of Capernaum that it would be more tolerable for Sodom on the day of judgement than it would be for them.

Youngsters growing up in a Christian home can sometimes wish they did not have to go to church. They resent be prevented doing things and going places their friends enjoy. They cannot see the immense privilege of having Christian parents who care enough for them to say no. To have parents who see them as a gift from God to be treasured and nurtured is a rich blessing.

There are those who go to church regularly and hear the gospel preached, but are not saved. They probably have family and friends who pray for them. They are exposed to God yet in their hearts they prefer Sodom.

Lot's wife had great privileges but she looked back longingly on Sodom. She preferred the Sodomite lifestyle to gospel privileges. The riches of grace were not riches to her and not as valuable as Sodom's sin. The blessings of God to her were a bind which opposed what her heart wanted. She was no thief and no adulteress, but God was shut out of her life and so she experienced the same judgement as Sodom's homosexuals. She looked back longingly and died. No wonder Jesus told us to remember Lot's wife.

The saddest thing about this woman is that she experienced judgement on the brink of salvation. Death came to her in the presence of mercy and she died with her hand in the hand of an angel. We need to remember Lot's wife because for many today the road to hell goes right through a gospel-preaching church. They hear the gospel regularly but never turn to Jesus. Of such people Jesus said that it will be more tolerable for Sodom on the day of judgement than for them.

# 7.

# Two kings
# — David and Manasseh

Psalm 23 speaks of David's experience of God and throughout there is an overwhelming sense of reality. It is clear that the psalmist is speaking of a God he knows, and in doing so he reveals the great joy in his heart brought about by the real and close communion he has with God. 'The Lord is my shepherd' speaks of nearness and involvement, of concern and dependence. It reveals to us what the Lord our God *can* be to every believer, and *ought* to be in the experience of all his people. This is more than mere formal religion and this is what the Bible means when it talks of sinners meeting God.

## The Lord

To appreciate fully the wonder of what David is saying, we need to see that the emphasis is on the word 'Lord', not 'shepherd'. It is who the Shepherd is that is remarkable. Who is David's shepherd? When in Scripture the title for God is in capital or small capital letters, as 'Lord' is here, it means that the original Hebrew word is Jehovah. This is the greatest title by which God revealed himself to man. Jehovah is the great name in which the Old Testament is always delighting. In Psalm 83 the psalmist says of the enemies of God, 'Let them know that you, whose name is the Lord [Jehovah] — that you alone are the Most High over all the earth' (v. 18). He is a God of all power, one not to be trifled with. Isaiah delights in the Lord as the high and lofty one, who lives for ever and whose name is holy (Isaiah 57:15). This is the same Jehovah that Paul calls the eternal King (1 Timothy 1:17), and the eternal God (Romans 16:26).

Throughout the Old and New Testaments the Lord is represented as the one who created the universe out of nothing and upholds it with the word of his own power and the strength of his own hand. This is Jehovah, and this great and glorious creator of the universe has graciously condescended to draw near to David and to all his people.

## Shepherd

In the Old Testament the job of shepherd was a most menial one. If a man had several sons it was the youngest who looked after the sheep. David himself was the youngest of Jesse's sons and that was why he was a shepherd. What right had David, or any of us, to call the holy sovereign God his shepherd? Indeed, is it not something of a comedown to refer to so majestic and awesome a being in this way? The answer to both questions is that the title of Shepherd is one that the LORD had given to himself! David did not invent it, nor did he refer to his LORD as Shepherd because he himself happened to be a shepherd. If he had been a fisherman or a shopkeeper, he would have still used this title, because from the earliest times in Scripture the LORD had revealed himself to his people under the picture of a shepherd.

In Genesis 49:24 we find the dying Jacob speaking to his children and reminding them that their God is the Shepherd, and Rock of Israel. Isaiah, in chapter 40, is likewise reminding Israel who their God is. There is always the tendency to forget the greatness of the LORD, and twice the prophet rebukes the people: 'Do you not know? Have you not heard?' (vv. 21 & 28). He then paints a marvellous picture of the greatness of God as the one who sits upon the circle of the earth and before whom the nations are like a drop in a bucket. In the midst of these thrilling words the LORD is described as tending his flock like a shepherd (v. 11).

Ezekiel tells us that there are false shepherds who would lead the people of God astray. Nevertheless, the LORD says, 'I myself will search for my sheep and look after them' (34:11). Then God goes on to say, 'I will place over them one shepherd, my servant David, and he will tend them; he will tend them and be their shepherd' (v. 23). The David in this verse is not the king who wrote Psalm 23, but David's greater son, the Lord Jesus Christ. Ezekiel is prophesying of the coming of the Messiah, as too is Zechariah when he says, 'Awake, O sword, against my shepherd ... "Strike the shepherd, and the sheep will be scattered"' (13:7). The day before Jesus went to Calvary, he quoted this verse, applying it to his death on the cross (Matthew 26:31).

## The Good Shepherd

The title that David uses to describe his relationship with God was no chance expression arising out of his own particular background. It was a divinely ordained title and there was only one who possessed the right to it. The title was claimed by Jesus when in John 10 he described himself as the Good Shepherd. And the Holy Spirit exclusively applied the title to Jesus when he inspired the writer of Hebrews to call the Saviour the great Shepherd (13:20) and the apostle Peter to refer to Jesus as the Chief Shepherd (1 Peter 5:4).

Jesus is the promised Messiah. He is Jehovah, the Lord God, who became flesh at Bethlehem. The Old Testament writers delight in God as their Shepherd and this picture finds its fulfilment in the Lord Jesus Christ. Jesus is our Shepherd. The one who died on the cross did so as our Shepherd giving his life for the sheep. From the beginning of time Jesus is the only Shepherd of God's flock. He is the self-existing, uncreated, eternal Jehovah whose love and care, providence and power are unlimited and inexhaustible. This is why Christians always need to be diligent in maintaining the doctrine of the person of Christ. He is no mere man, but God incarnate. If Jesus is not God, then he is not our Shepherd. And if he is not our Shepherd, then we are lost, both now in this world and for all eternity in hell. But Jesus is God. He is Jehovah. He is our Shepherd, and his Shepherd care extends over all time and eternity. He is the Shepherd to all the saints in every generation, supplying their need, anticipating every emergency, and ensuring the happiness and security of every single member of the flock.

## Dependable

The Shepherd has the ultimate responsibility for the flock. If he is to lead it into green pastures, he has to first find those pastures. The same is true about the quiet or still waters. So the flock has to depend for its very existence and survival upon the Shepherd. Is such a dependence justified? Yes, it is totally justified because the Shepherd is Jesus. In strength he is almighty, in wisdom he is omniscient, in love he is unequalled, and in resources he is unbounded. There are no evils that he cannot deal with; no dangers that he cannot avert; no enemy that he cannot defeat; and no needs that he cannot supply.

No wonder David delights in his Shepherd and the same is true of all believers. All we need we can find in Jesus. To the troubled heart he can bring peace, to the weary rest, to the penitent pardon, to the weak strength. Christians lose so much of the joy of salvation by concentrating on what they can do for the Shepherd instead of on what the Shepherd has done and continues to do for them.

The flock is the constant object of his love. He knows every sheep and lamb by name. No human shepherd could be like that. But Jesus has our names engraved on the palms of his hands. There is not a second when his eye wavers from us, not a moment when his prayers and intercession desert us. He sees us all as individuals and loves us with an everlasting love. Therefore the greatest privilege any human being can have is to know Jesus as their Shepherd.

'The Lord is my Shepherd' is an amazing statement and everything else in Psalm 23 follows on as an inevitable consequence of it. This is not some theoretical proposition. It is not wishful thinking: it is far more even than just a theological statement. This is the experience of all God's people. This is what we are saved to, and the reality of what we are saved to is known as we submit to the care of the Shepherd. It is no use saying 'the Lord is my Shepherd', and then worrying myself sick about where I am going to find green pastures. If the green pastures and quiet waters are found as a result only of our efforts, we do not need a Shepherd. But the fact is that we make a terrible mess of life, and we *need* Jesus to be our Shepherd.

## Manasseh

In the Old Testament Israel and Judah had very few good kings. This is exactly what God had predicted when the people first asked for a king. One of the few exceptions was Hezekiah. In his reign he turned the nation back to God and the spiritual quality of his life was such that the Bible says, 'Hezekiah trusted in the Lord, the God of Israel. There was no one like him among all the kings of Judah, either before him or after him. He held fast to the Lord and did not cease to follow him; he kept the commands the Lord had given Moses. And the Lord was with him' (2 Kings 18:5-7).

The strange and sad thing is that this godly man produced a son, Manasseh, who was by far the worst king Judah had. Some have called him the wickedest man who ever lived. As we read of Manasseh in the Old Testament books of 2 Kings and 2 Chronicles it is not difficult to see why he has earned this terrible description.

## His reign

Manasseh was only twelve years old when his father died and he became king. It was not long before he undid all the good Hezekiah had worked for. We are told he restored idolatry; God's temple was given over to idol worship; the people were forbidden to worship the Lord; scriptures were destroyed; human sacrifice was practised; and the result of all this was that 'Manasseh led Judah and the people of Jerusalem astray, so that they did more evil than the nations the LORD had destroyed before the Israelites' (2 Chronicles 33:9).

The enormity of the godlessness and sin of this man is beyond our understanding. The Bible says, 'He sacrificed his own son in the fire, practised sorcery and divination, and consulted mediums and spiritists. He did much evil in the eyes of the LORD, provoking him to anger' (2 Kings 21:6).

This went on for nearly fifty years so there grew up in the land a generation who never knew what it was to worship the LORD and who were never taught the Word of God. All this was due to this one man Manasseh.

## God's reaction

While all this was going on God was not indifferent. He saw it all and was angry. God was angry with Manasseh for rejecting the faith of his father and for leading the people astray. He was angry with the people for following Manasseh's evil ways. Sin always provokes God to anger. He cannot look indifferently upon it. His holiness will always react against evil. This is true whether it be the evil sin of Manasseh or our so-called respectable sins of pride, envy and gossip. We must not make the mistake of thinking that it was only the enormity of Manasseh's sin that aroused God's anger. All sin has the same effect. Isn't this what Jesus said in the Sermon on the Mount? Murder or gossip, adultery or evil thoughts, it is all the same. It is all rebellion against God and the end of it will also be the same judgement of hell.

However, although God is angry with Manasseh we find that once again he is a God slow to anger and plenteous in mercy. He spoke through his prophets to the people urging repentance and warning of the consequence if they did not: 'I will wipe out Jerusalem as one wipes out a dish' (2 Kings 21:13).

But they would not listen. It has ever been the same. Jesus wept over Jerusalem and declared that he wanted to protect them like a hen protects her chicks, but they would not heed him.

Manasseh would not listen so God acts in judgement. He allows the Assyrians to conquer Judah, and Manasseh is led away in chains with a hook in his nose (2 Chronicles 33:11). He would have been paraded through the streets, mocked and eventually left to rot in prison. We would probably say that he deserved all that he got and would have had little sympathy for him.

## Repentance

So Manasseh is in prison in Babylon with no friends and no sympathy. But a strange thing happened. He begins to pray, and not to the idols he had worshipped for the past fifty years, but to the LORD. The Bible says he 'humbled himself greatly before the God of his fathers' (2 Chronicles 33:12). He thinks and ponders on his life, on the twelve years when his father taught him by word and example about the LORD. He thought about God speaking to him through the prophets, and he thought about his sin and his continual rejection of God.

Have you ever done that? Have you reviewed your life and God's dealings with you? Maybe you are like thousands who had Christian parents but you rejected all they stood for. This man thought long and seriously and he came to the conclusion that he had been completely wrong. He now knew that there is only one true God, so he cries to him for mercy.

We might be tempted to say that we have seen all this before. Trouble comes so people turn to God, and when the trouble goes God is forgotten. Our scepticism would probably have rejected Manasseh. I wonder how most of us would have dealt with this evil man? He had done so many evil things but now he is grovelling in front of us. Would you forgive him?

God did, and God is no soft touch. God knows the heart of man so he cannot be fooled. If we were to be judged by each other there would be little hope for any of us. But the God of grace and mercy is our judge. He knows if the repentance is genuine, and God forgave Manasseh. The amount of sin or the type of sin does not affect whether or not we can be forgiven. The important thing is that there is true repentance, genuine sorrow for sin and a real faith in Christ.

God forgave Manasseh and gave him back his throne. This is how great and complete God's salvation is. The hymnist says that we are ransomed, healed, restored and forgiven. But perhaps the greatest thing about this story of Manasseh is the proof that God's mercy far outweighs his wrath. There never was a man who more deserved hell and less deserved heaven than Manasseh; but God's salvation has nothing to do with what we deserve. It is all of grace.

If God could save this man, he can save you.

# 8.

# Only one way

John 14:6 says very clearly and plainly that there is only one way to come to God: 'Jesus answered, "I am the way and the truth and the life. No one comes to the Father except through me."' This is not bigotry or intolerance, but is founded on basic biblical reasons.

1. *Because it is God's work.* It is God who is providing the way and what God does he does perfectly first time. If we were doing it we would never get it right and would have to make improvement all the time.

2. *For our peace of mind.* If there were more than one way we would never be sure that we had found the best way. We have the best way because there is only one way.

3. *Because of the nature of salvation.* Salvation is from sin but man does not understand his sin. Therefore he cannot understand salvation. Man sees sin as a social blip, a temperamental hiccup, and not as a direct attack

upon the person and integrity of God. He does not view it as a violation of God's law; nor as a contradiction to all that God stands for. Sin like this needs an infinite power to overcome it and only God can supply such a power.

4. *Because of the cost involved.* The cost was so enormous that even God with his infinite resources could not have provided it twice. It took all that God had.

Imagine a man whose only child was dying of some terrible illness. The only cure is a very expensive operation. It cannot be done on the National Health Service; it can only be done in America. But the cost is huge.

To pay the cost he sells all he has and mortgages his house. All the money he raises goes to pay for the operation. This is his only child so everything is sacrificed. But if the one needing the operation was not his child but his enemy, would he still do it? If the one in need hated him, lied about him, scorned him — would he still do it? NO. But that is exactly what God did.

## The world hates this way

A world that can tolerate just about anything — homosexuality, lesbianism, abortion — cannot tolerate the fact that there is only one way to God. Of all things about the

Christian faith, what the world hates most is the teaching about the uniqueness and exclusiveness of Jesus.

Jesus said, '[The world] hates me,' (John 7:7). How can the world hate the most loving and gentle man who ever lived? How can it hate a Jesus so gracious, merciful, compassionate?

Jesus tells us in the same verse — because he tells them that what they do is evil; or, in other words, because they are wrong and that he is the only way to God.

Their religion is wrong; their morals are wrong; their philosophy is wrong. The world hates authority, particularly absolute authority that allows for no alternative. A philosopher is a man who tells you what he thinks. He has spent his whole adult life in or around universities; he has umpteen degrees; he has written books and so he tells us what he thinks about God. But what he thinks about God has no more worth than what a road sweeper thinks about God.

We need to hear what God has to say, which means we need to listen to the Bible. But the world hates the Bible because it teaches of only one way to God. The one way is always God's way. This is anathema to unbelievers and that is why evolutionists can say with no shame or embarrassment that although they can never prove evolution to be true the only alternative is creationism, and they will not have that.

*I want to show you that the only way to God is Jesus, and that this is reasonable.*

A young woman in her mid-twenties came into the church one Sunday for the first time. After the service I spoke to her and discovered she was a schoolteacher and a very devout Roman Catholic. 'If you are a Roman Catholic,' I said, 'why have you come here?' She answered, 'I know God but I know nothing about Jesus. I want to learn about Jesus.' I replied, 'You cannot know God without Jesus.' She was amazed at the answer, as many religious people would be; but the Bible is very clear that Jesus is the only way to God.

Given the religious thought of today this truth is unacceptable to many. They regard it as bigoted and a failure to recognize the worth of religions other than Christianity. The prevailing thought is that everyone is entitled to his opinion and that one religious opinion is as good as the next. A more unreasonable and absurd attitude it would be difficult to find. How can several diametrically opposed teachings concerning the way to God all be right? It is like a man in Edinburgh asking the way to London and being given the conflicting instructions to take a plane and fly west, take a boat and go east, and take a train and go south. If he has any sense he will know that all the answers cannot be right. If he takes the trouble to look at a map he will be able to decide which piece of advice he should follow.

Accepting the truth that Jesus is the only way to God is not intolerant bigotry; it is simply believing the teaching God has given us in his Word. There Jesus said, 'I am the way and the truth and the life. No one comes to the Father except through me' (John 14:6). Peter said, 'Salvation is found in no one else, for there is no other name under heaven given to men by which we must be saved' (Acts 4:12).

Paul said, 'For there is one God and one mediator between God and men, the man Christ Jesus' (1 Timothy 2:5). Nothing is stated more clearly in the Bible. The above quotes can bear no interpretation other than that Jesus is the only way to God.

## The problem

The way to God and heaven is shut to us by our sin. That sin must be dealt with to God's satisfaction if a way is to be opened for sinners. Sin is a breaking of God's law and a rebellion against the authority of God. It is not merely a moral defect but an affront to the character and holiness of the Lord. Sin is a serious business and God's reaction to it is revealed in Genesis 6:5-6: 'The LORD saw how great man's wickedness on the earth had become, and that every inclination of the thoughts of his heart was only evil all the time. The LORD was grieved that he had made man on the earth, and his heart was filled with pain.'

God cannot be indifferent to sin and his opposition to it is not just that of a judge. His heart is the heart of a loving father pained and grieved by the waywardness of his children. For him to say that he was sorry he ever made man is a staggering acknowledgement. When man sins, God suffers.

Human sin affects the relationship between God and man in two basic ways. Firstly, it brings upon us the wrath and condemnation of God. Secondly, it leaves us totally unable to meet God's requirements of love and obedience to his law and word. If a way is to be opened to God it must deal with both these problems. The way to God must be one that meets with God's full approval and satisfies the demands of God's law. Sin must be dealt with if we are ever to have a happy relationship with God. This problem is immense. It is completely beyond man to solve even though history is full of his perverted ingenuity to obtain divine favour. If there is to be a solution, it is God who must provide it.

## God's remedy

In John 3:16 we have a perfect statement of God's remedy for sin: 'For God so loved the world that he gave his one and only Son, that whoever believes in him shall not perish but have eternal life.' In his divine love God provides a remedy which deals justly with the punishment that sin deserves and yet at the same time provides pardon for the sinner. God has said that the penalty for sin is death — spiritual and physical death. Nothing can change that because it is the judgement of the holy God. God will not turn a blind eye to our sin. Justice must be done, so the demands of God's law and the penalty for breaking that law must be satisfied.

In love and mercy God declares that he will accept a substitute to die in the sinner's place. But God's law demands that the substitute must be free from the guilt of sin and therefore not deserving of death himself. None of us could meet these requirements. So God sent his own Son into the world to become man and to keep his law fully and perfectly. This is what the man Jesus did, and thus became the only acceptable sacrifice to God for human sin. This is why Jesus is the only way to God.

## No other way

In John 14:6, the verse quoted at the beginning of this chapter, Jesus is not saying that he is one of many ways to God but that he is the *only way*. There is a uniqueness and exclusiveness about Jesus when it comes to the matter of our salvation. There is a triple claim in that verse which is quite amazing. Jesus is *the* way and *the* truth and *the* life. There is no alternative to him and the second part of the verse confirms this: 'No one comes to the Father except through me.'

Why is Jesus so adamant that he is the only way to God? The stand he is taking leaves him either totally deluded or totally correct. There is no room for half measure. Either

Jesus is deluded and we can safely ignore him, or he is right and therefore it would be the greatest possible folly to ignore him. Our eternal destiny hangs upon this. So do we believe that Jesus is the only way to God?

## What alternative do you have?

Because of its hatred of one-way Christianity the world has spent the past 2000 years looking for an alternative to Jesus. Self-effort, morality, all sorts of variations of Christianity and every conceivable alternative religion have been put forward. Renowned people such as Prince Charles have supported this and if he becomes the next king of Great Britain he has said that he does not want to be known as Defender of *the* Faith, but Defender of Faith.

All this effort has been useless in man's search for God, so at last the final answer has apparently been found — man decides there is no God, so we do not need a way to him.

But when man has made all his pronouncements about life, death and eternity, there still remains the great unalterable fact of GOD. And there is still only one way to know this God.

There is no alternative to Jesus. That is where you are now. It is either Jesus or hell. What a choice! In all the choices you have to make in life, none is as clear and obvious as this.

# 9.

# Nicodemus

John chapter three is probably one of the most well-known chapters in the Bible. Most Christians could give an accurate account of the conversation between Jesus and Nicodemus, and most could repeat the sixteenth verse from memory. Here we find Jesus and the Pharisee having an earnest and serious conversation, and Jesus proceeding to teach this man what is one of the most basic doctrines of the Christian faith — the doctrine of regeneration, of being born again.

A man can be ignorant of many things in the Bible and still be saved; but J. C. Ryle says, 'To be ignorant of the matters handled in this chapter is to be on the broad way which leads to destruction.'

We do not become Christians as a result of Bible knowledge or of understanding theology; but Jesus says if we are to be Christians we must be born again. There are not different categories of Christians: those born again, and those not born again. We cannot become Christians at all without this new birth. When Jesus said 'must', he meant there was no alternative. This is why this chapter is so important.

Basically, the chapter tells us of one man alone with Jesus. Here is one individual in the presence of the Saviour. The next chapter speaks of a woman who had a similar experience. Intellectually, morally and socially, the man and the woman were poles apart, but what they had in common, namely an encounter with Jesus, was of far more importance and of lasting consequence than anything else that was true of them. The whole purpose of the Christian gospel is to bring men and women to Jesus. We all need a personal encounter with the Saviour and the message of the gospel is that it is just as possible for us as it was for Nicodemus.

## The Pharisee

The first verse gives us the formal details of this man. Nicodemus was a Pharisee, a member of the Jewish ruling council. He was a religious leader and teacher, as is made clear in verse ten. He was a man of prominence in the community. The Pharisees were a very strict religious group who bitterly opposed Jesus. Almost every reference to them in the New Testament finds them contradicting him. It was this group who, along with the priests, took a major role in planning his death. Although they were very religious Jesus called them hypocrites, 'like white-washed sepulchres [stone caskets]': all nice and clean on the outside but on the inside 'full of dead men's bones'.

The Pharisees were very much a 'salvation by works' party. They could not understand Christ's message of grace, of the free unmerited gift of God, for they had reduced the glorious God-given religion of the Jews to a set of man-made laws, many of which were quite ridiculous. This was especially true about their Sabbath laws. For example, a woman was not permitted to look in a mirror on the Sabbath because she might see a grey hair and be tempted to pull it out, which would be considered working; and an egg laid on the Sabbath could only be eaten if you killed the hen.

As Nicodemus belonged to this religious group, what was he doing coming to Jesus? Was he beginning to see the emptiness of his religion? It is clear in verse 2 that he had heard and seen something of the ministry of Jesus. Was he now beginning to see how ineffective was the man-made religion of the Pharisees, compared to this man's teaching?

Man is a strange and ingenious creature who has created many wonderful things in this world; but he has also created many evil things. Of all man's creations nothing is as vile and evil as man-made religion. Whether it be Phariseeism, Hinduism, Islam or the many distortions of Christianity, the result of man-made religion is always to reduce God to our size, to make God manageable. And it is always a 'salvation by works' religion. Consequently it takes men away from God. It leaves men and women with no Saviour and no answer to their sin and guilt.

The nonsense of Phariseeism is clear to see, but do we see how equally ridiculous is much of man-distorted Christianity? For instance, does the sprinkling of a few drops of water on a baby's head really make it a Christian? Does going to church now and again, or even every week, make a sinner right with God? Isn't that as ridiculous as the Pharisees' grey hair and the egg? Is it not reducing the glorious faith of Jesus to an empty formalism? Is this all we understand by biblical Christianity? Is it merely enough to call ourselves Methodists or Baptists, Catholics or Anglicans, or even Evangelicals? Is that all that God requires of us? Or are you beginning to see the emptiness of all man-made religion? Are you questioning your so-called faith and asking 'Is this all there is?' Are you beginning to long for a real experience of God, something more than religion is giving you? What does your religion do for you in the stress of work during the week? How does your religion cope with suffering and death? Does it have an answer that really satisfies you and leaves you with peace and hope?

## No hope

Man-made religion will always leave a person where it left Nicodemus. According to Jesus in verse 3 it left Nicodemus with no hope of seeing heaven and therefore on the way to hell. If he continued as he was — good, respectable, religious, moral — he would never see heaven. Imagine what that would mean for this man whose whole life was steeped in religion! So why did Jesus say this? Because man-made religion has no answer to man's greatest problem, which is sin. Man's greatest problem is that because of his sin he is unacceptable to the holy God. And in this chapter Jesus says that the consequence of our *sin* is that we perish (v. 16) and are already under the just condemnation of God (v. 18). Man-made religion will always leave us without God and without hope in this world (Ephesians 2:12).

## Confusion

It will also leave us in a state of total confusion and bewilderment as to spiritual truths. When Jesus speaks to Nicodemus of man's most basic and fundamental need in his relationship to God, the need for a new birth, the need to be born again, Nicodemus is totally confused (see v. 4). He cannot understand spiritual concepts and he interprets them in a literal way that makes them appear nonsense. This is a religious teacher and Jesus has exploded a theological bomb in his mind — 'you must be born again.' This bombshell shatters Nicodemus and he totters in utter confusion and misunderstanding (v. 4).

It is still the same when religious people are confronted with basic biblical doctrines on how to become a Christian. When a person who has been taught all his life that Christianity is simply a matter of doing your best, caring for the poor and starving, and going to church now and again, hears the true gospel, it is so revolutionary, so new, so strange, that it explodes in his mind causing a cross between bewilderment and panic. All sorts of counter questions flood into his mind which are as irrelevant and absurd as those of Nicodemus: 'Surely he cannot enter a second time into his mother's womb to be born!'

What Nicodemus is doing is not thinking but reacting in such a way as to shut out the truth of the gospel. Many still do the same thing. To them Jesus says, as he did to Nicodemus, THINK! Christianity never bypasses a man's mind. It demands that we think, that we apply our minds as well as our hearts to God's truth. Here he goes on to explain exactly what it means to be born again and why it is so essential.

## Emptiness

Here then is a man with plenty of formal religion but with no real experience of God. So what brings him to Jesus? Perhaps it was an awareness of the emptiness of his life, which his own religion was not filling. It could not — no more than drink or drugs or a hectic round of social activities can fill and satisfy. The empty life is empty because it lacks God. Nicodemus had his fill of religion and he probably had many friends, enough money and plenty of things to do and places to go — but still his life was empty. Then in his emptiness he comes into contact with Jesus. He first hears of Jesus, then he observes him, and he is impressed. Nicodemus seems to be going through life quite happily with his religion, but he does not know anything better. What he has is clearly superior to the religion he sees in foreigners but really he is living in the confines of his man-made religion. But then he hears of Jesus. He cannot understand everything about Jesus but two things stand out and he mentions them in verse 2.

The teaching and power of Jesus are so extraordinary that there is only one possible explanation — God is with him. So he has a very high estimation of Jesus. What do you think of Jesus? Do you regard him as a great man, an exceptional man? Do you have a lofty and high view of Jesus?

Jesus once asked his apostles, 'Who do people say the Son of Man is?' (Matthew 16:13); in other words, 'What is the current, popular opinion of me?' The answer was somewhat encouraging. Some people said Jesus was John the Baptist come back from the dead. Others said he was Elijah or Jeremiah. All these were great and exceptional men, but of course these opinions were wrong and all pitiably inadequate. It is possible to have a very high estimation of Jesus and still be wrong.

Who is Jesus? He is God. He is Emmanuel, God with us. So then his teaching is the Word of the living God and when Jesus says you *must* be born again, you *must*.

Are you?

Our response to the teaching of Jesus will always be conditioned by whether or not we believe Jesus is the Son of God. This is made very clear in John chapter six. Here were people with a very high opinion of Jesus and they were prepared to take up arms and make him king (vv. 14-15). Yet when he begins to teach them basic Christian doctrine their reaction in verse 60 is 'This is a hard teaching. Who can accept it?', and they leave Jesus and no longer follow him (v. 66). The reason for this is that though they were greatly impressed with Jesus they saw him as no more than a man (see v. 42).

Compare this estimation with that of a true believer in verse 69: 'We believe and know that you are the Holy One of God.' If you believe that, then you must take him seriously when he says that in order to be Christians, *we must be born again.*

# 10.

# The Ethiopian eunuch

The story of the conversion of the Ethiopian eunuch shows us the deep concern God has for an individual soul. It also shows that there are no accidents when God is at work. It is very clear from Acts 8 that the meeting of preacher and seeker was planned by God. He took Philip out of revival in Samaria into the desert to meet this man in whose life he had been working for a long time.

Is this true in every conversion? Yes, to a greater or lesser degree. Every conversion is a result of the grace and love of God, and each soul is dealt with as an individual. We are all saved one at a time. Hence every conversion is carefully planned by God. Circumstances and the people involved are ordered by God. Nothing is by chance. This truth is both humbling and thrilling.

The Ethiopian was an intelligent man with a very responsible job — 'an important official in charge of all the treasury of Candace, queen of the Ethiopians' (Acts 8:27). He was highly respected. He was trusted and admired; yet he was also dissatisfied. This is obvious from the fact that he had been to Jerusalem to worship. Why go all that way? Ethiopia had plenty of gods. In fact the king there was worshipped as a child of the sun and regarded as too sacred to perform secular functions of royalty. These were done by the queen mother Candace.

He had 'tried' all the gods available and if you were to ask this man whether all religions were the same, he would have said that they were. None of them satisfied the longing of his heart. Here was a man looking for something and religion was not offering any answer.

There are many like that today. They know deep in their soul that there is a God and they want to know him. So they try one religion after another, but to no avail. They may even try different versions of Christianity. Yet still they are not satisfied.

Why? Because what they need is for someone to tell them about Jesus — the real Jesus. Not the effeminate, weak Jesus of modern Christianity, but the real Jesus of the Bible — the Jesus of the cross, who bore our sin and faced the wrath of God instead of us.

The Ethiopian had gone thousands of miles looking for God but now at last he was in the place where he was to hear of Jesus. No one finds God apart from Jesus. He is the only way to God.

That being the case, therefore:

• It was no coincidence that at Jerusalem he had been able to obtain a copy of the book of Isaiah;

- It was no coincidence that he was reading chapter 53, verse 32;
- It was no coincidence that at that moment he met a preacher who could tell him that Isaiah was speaking of Jesus.

Now let's be clear about this. Here was a man seeking God. *You* are to seek God. God commands you to do this. His Word says that we are to seek the Lord while he may be found. This man had done what he could do, but it was not enough. Perhaps he was feeling frustrated; it all seemed a waste of time.

Are you like that? You know you are not a Christian. You want to be a true believer, but you seem as far away now as ever. Be encouraged by the Ethiopian eunuch. God was at work. We do not find God; he finds us. But we must continue to seek.

Perhaps he came back from Jerusalem thinking it was all another wasted trip. Was it worth it? Should he bother again? Where should he go next? Which god should he try now? Some leave church like that on Sundays: confused, bewildered and dejected.

You say you want to know God. That is good. But let me ask you this: what are you reading? The Ethiopian was not reading a newspaper or a novel. His nose was in the word of God. True, he found it hard going; but he was looking in the right place. This was the place where his search would find its glorious completion.

## Why is this important?

This is vitally important because if you are to become a Christian it has to be in God's way. God's way is through Jesus his Son, and you find Jesus in the Bible. Philip's message to this seeking man concerned this Jesus of the Scriptures. He told the Ethiopian about the Jesus of whom Isaiah 53 speaks: the Jesus of the Bible — not the Jesus of men's imagination; not the Jesus invented by modern theology. We need to be aware that there is a Jesus spoken of today that bears no resemblance to the real Jesus.

Yet the Jesus of the Bible was sent by God, as the prophet Isaiah makes plain. Isaiah lived 700 years before Jesus, so how could he write about him? There is only one answer to that — God told him. The Old Testament is full of Jesus. Jesus did not just appear out of nowhere; for hundreds of years God had spoken in the Old Testament through the prophets, saying he was going to send the Messiah.

God always had a plan to save men and women from the consequences of their sin. That plan never changed — it was always through Jesus. The law of the Old Testament was never able to save; its function was to convict of sin — to show us we needed a Saviour. It was a schoolmaster to bring us to Christ. Because Jesus was sent by God we can be sure that he is perfectly qualified to be our Saviour. *He was the Jesus who died in our place.*

Here is the heart of the gospel and Isaiah spells it out clearly. The whole picture is one of suffering. Listen to the words used here — he was stricken, smitten, afflicted, pierced, crushed, punished, wounded, oppressed.

That is a frightening list. What did Jesus do to deserve this? Verse 9 says he had done no violence and there was no deceit in him. So surely he will plead his innocence. No, 'He was oppressed and afflicted, yet he did not open his mouth; he was led like a lamb to the slaughter, and as a sheep before her shearers is silent, so he did not open his mouth' (53:7).


## Why did it happen?

The answer to this is so staggering that most people refuse to believe it. Some say it is immoral. Impossible. Yet Isaiah states the answer very clearly and gets abundant support from the rest of scripture. Why did it happen? Listen to verses 4 and 10: 'Yet we considered him stricken by God'; 'It was the Lord's will to crush him and cause him to suffer.' It was God's will. God not only allowed all this to happen to his Son but God actually did it.

The death of Jesus, not only the act but also the way he died, was all part of God's plan. The plan is unfolded in chapter 53 for no less than ten times we are told that Jesus died *for* us, *instead* of us (vv. 4-6). Jesus did not suffer on account of any wrong he had done, but on behalf of his people. That is why there was no objection from him.

To say that Jesus died in the place of sinners is not enough. The Bible will not leave it there. It uses key words like 'propitiation' and 'blood' to describe what Jesus was doing on the cross.

So Isaiah did not leave it there. He describes how Jesus is crushed (v. 5) by the law and justice of God. Note the word crushed. This is much stronger than bruised, the word used in the Authorised Version of the Bible. A bruise is uncomfortable and leaves a mark. Crushing is agonizing and destroys. The Hebrew word for this is *daka,* and it is used to describe people being trampled to death. This is the death of Jesus.

## The reason

The reason for all this is given in verse 10: 'The Lord makes his life a guilt offering.' The language is that of the Old Testament sacrificial system. Simply, it means that if the guilty sinner is to be pardoned he must first produce a sacrifice, a spotless innocent victim to die in his place. This did two things. It showed the man acknowledged his sin and came trusting in God's way to make atonement for his sin. The wonder of the gospel is that God now makes his Son an offering for our sin. He sacrifices not innocent animals but his own Son. Jesus becomes the Lamb of God who takes away our sin.

Is this possible? Could it really happen? If in one of our courts a man is found guilty and sentenced to thirty years in prison, could someone else take his punishment instead of him? No. The law would not allow it. It would not be fair. But thank God that he allows it. We would have no hope otherwise. It is not fair that Jesus should die for guilty sinners, but fairness does not enter into it. It is not fair but it is just. This is so because God laid our sins on Jesus. He became responsible for them and paid the punishment they deserved.

This is what Philip told the Ethiopian. How did this man react to the gospel of Jesus?

## Remember his condition

The gospel told him why he had no peace. He was a sinner and there is no peace for the wicked. But it also told him God's answer to his sin. Jesus had died instead of him.

Do you believe that? Here is the only answer to your greatest problem. Jesus can make you acceptable to God.

The Ethiopian eunuch believed with all his heart. He had no arguments. He was guilty. Here was God's answer so he came unreservedly to Jesus for salvation. He would have been a fool not to.

# 11.

# If only

*If only* — two small words but they contain so much poignancy as they reflect the pain, anguish and bitterness locked up in the hearts of many people.

- *If only* the one I loved so much had not died so young;
- *If only* I had better health;
- *If only* I had said no when first offered drugs;
- *If only* I could have my time over again — things would be different now;
- *If only* I had more money;
- *If only*, if only, if only — words of regret, despair and hopelessness.

The problem with the 'if only' syndrome is that it cannot see beyond its own very limited sphere of vision. We lock ourselves into a painful 're-run' of events and wonder what might have been if things had turned out differently. The pain felt shuts us in to an inevitable hopelessness. It can see no solution and therefore expects no answer to its endless round of despair. And even when an answer is suggested, it is viewed with suspicion and disbelief.


## Nothing new

This state of mind is not a modern phenomenon. In the Old Testament book of Deuteronomy, God describes a people who had anxious minds and despairing hearts. He says of them, 'You will live in constant suspense, filled with dread both night and day, never sure of your life. In the morning you will say, "If only it were evening!" and in the evening, "If only it were morning!"' (Deuteronomy 28:66-67). Have you ever felt like this?

The reason for those people's state of mind was their rejection of God, and the answer was to turn back to God. But this is not always the case. Again in the Old Testament, a very good man named Job was forced by a series of adverse circumstances that were not of his making to cry out eight times, 'If only.' Such was his anguish that he said, 'If only I had never come into being' (Job 10:19). Then later when he realized that the answer was with God, he said, 'If only I knew where to find him; if only I could go to his dwelling!' (23:3).

What both Old Testament incidents teach us is that whatever the cause of our despair the answer is to be found in God. Job, in his misery, felt it was impossible to find God and maybe you feel the same way, but he was to discover this was not true. The good news is that Job did find the answer. His prayers were answered. He found God.

## God's 'if only'

Listen now to the 'if only' on the lips of God.

> 'I am the LORD your God, who teaches you what is best for you, who directs you in the way you should go. If only you had paid attention to my commands, your peace would have been like a river, your righteousness like the waves of the sea'
> (Isaiah 48:17-18).

All the problems of mankind, in whatever form they may manifest themselves, stem from a broken relationship with God. The Lord only seeks our good. He only wants what is best for us, but sin has blinded us to this truth. We see God's commands as restrictive and narrow, and therefore go our own way. The result is always devastating. 'If only' is the symptom of a heart complaining about the consequences of its own sin, or complaining about the effects of sin in general in the world.

## Real peace, no regrets

The answer to 'if only', is to know the reality of sin forgiven and peace with God through the Lord Jesus Christ. A temporary peace of mind can be found in many things, but lasting peace with God is found only in Jesus. This is possible because God sent his Son into the world to deal with our sin and guilt. This is what Jesus did on the cross when he accepted the responsibility for our sin and took the punishment those sins deserved. Peace with God is a product of salvation from sin.

When we know this peace, the 'if only' of despair is replaced with an assurance that God will never leave us and never take from us the salvation we have in Jesus.

You can know this peace
    by confessing your sin to God,
asking Him for forgiveness and
    trusting in Jesus alone
to make you acceptable to the Lord.

You need to see that the only answer is in the Lord Jesus Christ.

God did something amazing to deal with sin, and the good news of the gospel is that when Jesus died on the cross, he did so as the sinner's substitute. He stood in our place and took the punishment his people deserved. He died in our place, instead of us, and, by so doing, made it possible for God to forgive us all our guilt and sin.

## God's supreme act of love

The cross was God's supreme act of love and grace.

*At the cross,* we see God in all his divine holiness dealing with human sin — the terrorist's sin and our sin.

*At the cross,* God removed the sin that separates us from him by making his Son, the Lord Jesus, responsible for guilty sinners' violations of divine law.

*At the cross,* God credits our sin and guilt to Jesus, while crediting Jesus' righteousness to us.

*At the cross,* God's wrath fell on Jesus instead of us.

Many people ask why God doesn't do something about the evil in the world. They cannot see that he has done the greatest thing possible! Jesus has died for it and offers us salvation from it. Jesus satisfied all of God's requirements. Sin was punished as God prescribed it should be. There is now nothing further that divine justice can demand because Jesus has paid the debt in full.

Jesus is the only way of salvation because he alone is the way that God has provided for us. The Bible says of Jesus that 'Salvation is found in no one else, for there is no other name under heaven given to men by which we must be saved' (Acts 4:12). Jesus now says to you, 'Come to me, all you who are weary and burdened, and I will give you rest' (Matthew 11:28). He will deal with your sin and make you acceptable to God.

You come to Jesus by realizing that you are guilty and do not deserve pardon. But pardon is what you need. To 'come' means to believe in Jesus as God's only answer to deal with your sin. It means to trust what he did on your behalf on the cross and to look to him alone for forgiveness and salvation.

# 12.

# The rich young ruler

The story of the rich young ruler is told in the Gospels of Matthew, Mark and Luke, and it is one of the saddest stories in the Bible. It starts out so promisingly in Mark 10:17: 'As Jesus started on his way, a man ran up to him and fell on his knees before him. "Good teacher," he asked, "what must I do to inherit eternal life?"' but ends in the grief of verse 22: 'At this the man's face fell. He went away sad, because he had great wealth.'

Here is a young man who has all that the world can bestow on a youngster. He has the three things most men crave for — riches, youth and power. He also had a certain discernment and common sense because he knows that these things are only temporary. His youth will go inevitably and even if he can hang on to his riches and power they will only last as long as his body lasts. They are also temporary. He knows the truth of Job's words that we bring nothing into this world and we take nothing out.

Here was a young man who thinks. He knows what he has is but for a time and he desires something eternal. He wants something that will outlast his youth, riches and power. The sad thing is that he wants both his riches and eternal life. But at least here is a man thinking in terms of eternity, and that is rare. Most young men live for today. Some wiser ones plan for the future and seek to obtain academic qualifications, but even of these very few consider eternity. This is equally true of older folk as it is of the young. They are also bogged down in this world and live as if this is all there is.

Something else very important to see is that this young man knew he did not have eternal life otherwise he would not have asked about it. He did not fool himself with a false and groundless optimism about everything being alright in the end and everyone will go to heaven.

## Right question

He also knew that he could not buy, nor earn, nor demand eternal life. He asks how he could inherit it. He knew it had to be a gift. He was rich but no amount of money could get it for him. He was young but if he tried for the rest of his life he would never earn it. He was a ruler, a man of power, but even this could not help.

Eternal life is something outside of our ability or control. All we can do is ask. Are you clear about this? Many are not and seek to earn by their religion or morality what can only be obtained by asking.

But ask who? Here is another good thing about the rich young ruler; not only was he asking the right question but he was asking the right person. He had come to Jesus. Do you remember the words of Peter in John 6:68 when a large number of so-called disciples left Jesus and Jesus asked the twelve apostles if they were going to leave also. Peter replied, 'Lord, to whom shall we go? You have the words of eternal life.' The rich young ruler knew what Peter knew — only Jesus could help him.


## Right attitude

When he came to Jesus his attitude was right. He did not come in a patronizing manner, as if he was doing Jesus a favour. He did not come casually, as if it was of no real importance. But rather he came kneeling before Jesus, in humility and submission. Neither did he come reluctantly or hesitatingly. He came running, because he was anxious.

So he came, and we are told he was loved by Jesus. The heart of the eternal Son of God went out to this man, yet he went away without eternal life. He went away in great sadness.

How is it possible for this man to have all the positive qualities we have seen, for him to be loved by Jesus and yet still not be saved? We can well understand the apostles' dilemma: 'Who then can be saved?' (Mark 10:26).

## Why wasn't he saved?

The simple answer to this question is that he did not want to be saved. He was not interested in salvation and not even thinking about it. It is true that he asked about eternal life, but that is not the same as wanting to be saved. Eternal life is the result of salvation. It is the consequence of having one's sins forgiven. But as we shall see, this man had no awareness of his personal sin and guilt, therefore he could see no need of salvation. He wanted the product of salvation without the salvation itself. This is very important because many today are doing exactly the same thing.

There can be little doubt that if the apostles, understanding things as they did at that moment, had been left to deal with the rich young ruler he would not have gone away grieved. He would have gone away just as lost, but not grieved. They would probably have said that this was clearly the work of God. The man's attitude and his question would have encouraged them to believe he was now right with God.

If there is little doubt of that, there is no doubt that if the rich young ruler had been in a modern-day evangelistic crusade, when the appeal was made he would have gone forward and made a decision. As a result he would have gone home clutching a decision card which told him that he had eternal life.

## How did Jesus deal with him?

Jesus took this young man to the law of God. He took him to the Ten Commandments. This may seem strange to some and cause them to ask why Jesus did not apply grace to this seeker. It is grace that a lost soul needs. We may even be tempted to think that Jesus did not know how to lead a soul to salvation. Why the law? What was Jesus doing?

Paul gives us the answer in Galatians 3:24 when he tells us that the function of the law is to lead us to Christ. In the book of Romans Paul argues that if it were not for the law he would never have known he was a sinner and therefore never known he needed a Saviour.

When the young man was confronted with the Ten Commandments he says, in all seriousness and genuineness, that he had kept these all his life. An answer more full of darkness and self-ignorance it is not possible to imagine. It revealed that he knew nothing of the holiness of God nor of the sinfulness of his own nature. No man in whom the Holy Spirit is working would ever give such an answer.

There is much in this man to admire but he lacks the one thing essential to salvation, and that one thing is not an unwillingness to part with his money; that is merely a symptom. What he lacks is a conviction of sin. Because of this he sees no need to be saved and money then is more important than Jesus.

This man is not unique. There are many who want to go to heaven. They want eternal life but see no need of repentance. They treat God as an insurance man and go to church to pay their dues. God to them is a means to an end and they cannot see that God is the end as well as the beginning. Having no awareness of the greatness and holiness of God they can have no real awareness of their own sin. For people like the rich young ruler their respectability can be the greatest hindrance to salvation.

If you want eternal life then you have to be saved, and you cannot be saved without a conviction of sin and repentance.

# 13.

# The genuine and the fake

On a recent holiday to Spain I bought my wife a Rolex wristwatch. You will probably know that Rolex are one of the finest watches to possess and are very expensive. Before you think what a generous man I am and how fortunate my wife is, I ought to tell you that she also bought me a Rolex.

Two Rolex watches! That must have cost a fortune. No, not really; they only cost about £10 each because they were not genuine but fakes. But they were good fakes. If you held a genuine Rolex (which could cost up to £2000) and my £10 fake in your hand you would have great difficulty telling them apart. They look alike and they both keep perfect time. So what is the difference between the genuine and the fake? Obviously the cost, but the other main difference is in who made them. The genuine one is made in Switzerland by a craftsman, the fake is probably made in a country such as China by someone copying the original and using inferior materials.

I said that if you held the genuine and the fake in your hand you would not be able to tell the difference; but if you compared them in a year or so, the difference would be obvious. By then the fake would have lost its gleam, the poor materials used to make it would have become tarnished and the difference in the skill used to make them would be seen clearly. Since I bought my fake a friend told me he had also bought one and the following week the hands had fallen off.

So why did I buy a fake? One reason was that I could not afford the genuine article, but another reason was so that I could use this illustration.

There are many people who call themselves Christian but they are not genuine; they are fakes. They may be genuine in the sense that they really do think they are Christians, but none the less they are fakes. They look like Christians, talk like them and deceive a lot of people as well as themselves. So what is the difference? Like the Rolex watch it is the cost it took to buy them and who made them.


## God's workmanship

Genuine Christians are the product of the grace of God. In describing what a Christian is, Paul says in Ephesians 2:10: 'We are God's workmanship.'

In that same passage in Ephesians 2 Paul introduces three great gospel words which describe a genuine believer perfectly — love, mercy and grace. And they all speak of an activity of God. Not *our* works but *God's* works. Out of God's love flow mercy and grace. Mercy is God not giving us what we deserve. Grace is God giving us what we do not deserve.

All this is brought together in this amazing statement that the Christian is God's workmanship. We are the result of the work and activity of God. Listen again to Ephesians 2:10: 'For we are God's workmanship, created in Christ Jesus.' Notice that Paul uses the word 'created'. That is a powerful word and he uses it deliberately. As 2 Corinthians 5:17 says, 'If anyone is in Christ, he is a new creation.'

The word 'create' means that it is utterly and completely new; it had no previous existence. That little word shatters any illusion that my own efforts are able to make me a Christian. It also shows that when God was dealing with the problem of human sin he did not do a 'repair' job. He scrapped the original and made something new.

That is what a Christian is. He is not a repaired sinner. He is a new creation with a new nature. He was in Adam but now he is in Christ and that is only possible because we are God's workmanship.

Let us come back for a minute to my wristwatch. When you pay £10 for a Rolex you do not expect it to be genuine. For that price it has to be a fake. When you come across someone who is a Christian by their own efforts rather than by the grace of God, they too have to be a fake — a sincere fake, a kind fake, a generous fake; but none the less a fake. It takes divine love, grace and mercy to make the real thing.

## How does God the workman make Christians?

He starts by taking the raw material of human nature which is twisted and warped by sin and working on it. Men and women are dead in sin. This is the repeated emphasis of the New Testament. So we need life — spiritual life. This is why Jesus said that we must be born again. We cannot be a genuine Christian if we are not born again. The fake Christian does not understand the new birth. He thinks religion is enough but Jesus said that we *must* be born again.

God's love, like his holiness, destroys the myth that the sinner can save himself. The gospel starts with an activity of God, 'God so loved the world,' and then demands a response from man: 'whoever believes in him…' (John 3:16). The order is important. Man is called upon to respond to an action of God. The initiative is God's. If God had done nothing to save us, then nothing could be done. That is why being born again is so essential. If a person is not born again he or she is spiritually dead and cannot understand spiritual truths or respond to the grace and mercy of God. Being born again is God giving new life to a person who is dead in sin. This is a must; without it nothing else is spiritually possible, and it is the love of God that initiates it.

Our *response* to God would be impossible if God had not first of all shown love to us. John, in his first epistle, spells this out clearly for us: 'This is love: not that we loved God, but that he loved us and sent his Son as an atoning sacrifice for our sins'; 'We love because he first loved us' (1 John 4:10, 19).

## Love divine

God's love for us is not pity or sentiment, but intensely practical, because it motivates him to deal with our greatest problem. Man in sin is condemned already before the holy God (John 3:18). The sinner loves darkness; his deeds are evil; he hates the light (vv. 19-20). This puts him in the position of perishing (v. 16). It is clear from the illustration Jesus uses in verses 14 and 15 (see Numbers 21) that when he speaks of 'perishing' he means the judgement of God's wrath upon sin.

God deals with sin by giving his Son, the Lord Jesus Christ, to die for us. Jesus was made responsible for our sin and took its guilt and punishment. On the cross he faced the judgement and wrath of God that was due to his people.

That God should love us so much as to do this is staggering. It is love undeserved, and certainly unmerited, and as John has stressed in the verses quoted above from his epistle, it is love that was unsought by us. John also describes this love of God as being lavished upon us (1 John 3:1). 'Lavished' speaks of abundance, and tells us that God's love is no small thing, but a love unimaginable in its beauty and depth. It is this lavished love that enabled God to give his only Son to die instead of hell-deserving sinners.

## Our response

This love demands a response from us. The hymn 'When I survey the wondrous cross' by Isaac Watts says, 'Love so amazing, so divine, demands my soul, my life, my all.'

# 14.

# John the Baptist

John the Baptist was the cousin of Jesus but more importantly he had the God-given task of being the forerunner of the Christ. So pre-eminently he was a preacher and his preaching consisted of four elements — judgement, repentance, baptism and Christ.

It was his preaching of Christ that was by far the most important and gave purpose to the rest of his message. What is the only hope for a sinner under the judgement of God? — Christ. What is the use of repentance if there is no forgiveness of sins? — Christ forgives sin. Baptism is only the outward sign of a previous inward work of Christ in the heart. If we do not preach Christ everything else is meaningless and useless.

John saw his ministry solely in terms of Christ. He was to make way for the Christ. And even before he set eyes on Jesus he had a great love and reverence for him. He said of the coming Christ that he was not worthy to untie the thongs of his sandals. He also said, 'He must increase, but I must decrease' (John 3:30, AV).

This is why he preached Christ. His heart overflowed with love for God's Messiah and every opportunity was taken to point people away from himself and towards Christ. This man could so easily have revelled in his own popularity and in the crowds that flocked to hear him. His humility was produced by an exalted view of Christ. This is a lesson for all preachers of God's Word; and indeed for all Christians.

## What he preached about Christ

He spoke of Christ dealing with our sin. There were many other things he could have said but this is the message that thrilled his heart. The preaching that reaches the hearts of people is the message that has first thrilled the heart of the preacher. Heart reaches heart. One of the reasons for the cold, arid, negative preaching of so many evangelicals today is that they are not preaching Christ. They are not proclaiming how God deals in mercy with sin. It is one thing to preach sin and human guilt, but although this is necessary, it is quite another thing to preach how God deals with our sin in Christ.

It is one thing to mention that Christ died on our behalf, but it is quite another to delight in this, to proclaim it, expound it and convey the reality of it to sinners. No preacher can delight in Christ and be dry and boring. It is impossible.

## How he saw the work of Christ

He saw him as God's provision for our need. Christ is the Lamb of God. It is here that the sinner's hope and confidence is laid in the gospel. It tells us what God has done. Man is very clever and has achieved much. In this past century his accomplishments in science and medicine have been staggering, but he has no answer to human depravity and sin. He may have plenty of suggestions, but none that work!

So if all John the Baptist has to tell us is another religious theory, then he is wasting our time. But John speaks of what God has done. What authority does this man have that should make us listen to him?

First of all there was his own amazing birth. What happened to his father Zechariah at John's birth (Luke 1:57-66) proved that this baby was set aside by God for a very special ministry. Then at Jesus' baptism he saw the Holy Spirit descend upon Jesus. John knew what he was talking about.

If you had a great pain in your chest, causing you agony and distress, and I told you I had been talking to my butcher about you and he said the best cure for your pain is to eat fried lamb's liver, I do not think you would have much confidence in that. Nor if the man who services my central heating boiler advised that the best cure is to keep warm — so put on an extra woollen jumper. But if I told you to accompany me and speak to a friend who is the best cardiologist in the country — then you would have some hope.

Now take the problem of your sin — whatever form that sin may take: jealousy, pride, violence; all sin is a rejection of the word and ways of God. All sin is rebellion against God. It brings upon us the wrath of the Almighty God who has said that sin is so horrendous that it will take us to hell for eternity.

It is a very serious problem. So what is the answer? What is the remedy? It is no use looking to another sinner for an answer, whether that sinner is a butcher or a bishop. The only one to listen to is the God who is going to punish my sin. What does he say the answer is? Is not that a reasonable approach?

## God's answer

God's answer is very clear and he speaks it through his special servant John the Baptist. The remedy for your sin is Jesus Christ, the Lamb of God who takes away the sin of the world (John 1:29).

Clearly the phrase 'Lamb of God' is a special one and must have a meaning that is relevant to the problem of human sin and how God deals with it. What is equally clear is that throughout the Bible God deals with sin justly and mercifully, that is, in wrath and in love. God's justice cannot turn a blind eye to sin. He cannot sweep it under the carpet as if it is of no consequence.

The only way of dealing with sin justly is with the death of the sinner. The wages of sin is death. It would appear that God's justice leaves no room for mercy. It is because of this that the concept of Christ as the Lamb of God is crucial. It enables the justice of God to be fully satisfied and at the same time the love and mercy of God to be fully operative.

The Old Testament is full of references to this. For example, Jesus is the lamb of Leviticus 16, called the scapegoat; and he is the Passover Lamb of the Exodus.

These are but two of several references in Scripture to the coming Messiah or Christ, who is pictured as a lamb of sacrifice. The scapegoat represents the innocent dying in the place of the guilty. The Passover Lamb dies so that its blood can allow God to pass over in judgement when death comes to the land.

Then Revelation 7 looks forward to the work of the lamb but this time to the redeemed in heaven and they are there because they have washed their robes white in the blood of the Lamb.

So when John the Baptist says of Jesus, 'Look, the Lamb of God, who takes away the sin of the world!', he is saying that Jesus is God's answer to human sin. Jesus is to be the sacrifice who is provided by God and is therefore acceptable to God. When Jesus died on the cross he died in our place, as our substitute.

Since the creation of the world there have been billions and billions of people here, and every one of them a sinner.

The total amount of sin committed is beyond imagination. But God deems that the death of his Son is sufficient to atone for all that sin. This speaks volumes of the infinite worth of Jesus. One Jesus is enough to save a multitude, which no man can number, from an eternity in hell. Hallelujah, what a Saviour!

Let us now ask two questions. *How does Christ the Lamb of God take away our sin? Where does he take it to?*

## How Christ takes away our sin

To answer the first question we have to go back to Leviticus 16 and the scapegoat of the Day of Atonement. The Most Holy Place, or Holy of Holies, was the small room in the Tent of Meeting, or tabernacle, where the Ark of the Covenant was kept. The lid of the ark was called the mercy seat, and in this small room God's presence was deemed to be known in a special way. Therefore it was not to be entered lightly and only the high priest was allowed in, and then only once a year on the Day of Atonement. If the mercy seat was approached in God's prescribed way then there was great blessing for the people, but if it was approached in any other way, it meant death.

All this may sound very strange to us today but it was symbolizing two very important truths that are just as relevant now as they were in the days when Leviticus was written — namely, the unutterable holiness of God and the exceeding sinfulness of man. God wants us to come to him, but our sin is an enormous problem that must be dealt with first. The Old Testament system of sacrifices was instigated by God to remind man that his sin was a barrier. The sacrifice of bulls and goats and lambs was a symbolic way of cleansing the sinner that had one essential common factor: 'Without the shedding of blood there is no forgiveness' (Hebrews 9:22). They could not really deal with sin but served to remind the people of the fact of sin (Hebrews 10:3-4).

Several things took place on the Day of Atonement, but let us concentrate on the two goats mentioned in verses 7-10 of Leviticus 16. One was killed and its blood was taken by the high priest into the Most Holy Place and sprinkled on the mercy seat. This symbolized the turning away of the wrath of God from man's guilt. Mercy, instead of judgement, came upon the sinner.

The other goat, called the scapegoat, was brought to the high priest, who laid his hands on the animal's head and confessed the sins of the people. Symbolically the sins were transferred to the scapegoat and the goat, when sent into the desert, took away the sin of the people (vv. 20-22).

All this was symbolic. They were, says Hebrews 9:10, 'external regulations applying until the time of the new order'. That new order came with the Lord Jesus Christ. What was symbolic on the Day of Atonement became reality in Christ. The death of our Saviour is the only sacrifice that

God now recognizes. When Jesus died on the cross he did what both goats symbolized: he turned away the wrath of God from us and he took away our sin. Christ's sacrifice was once for all (Hebrews 10:10).

When men approach God today the only way that is acceptable to the holy God is through the Lord Jesus Christ. We must know that he has dealt once and for all with our sin; only then can we come with confidence into the presence of God.

Isaiah said in chapter 53 that God laid our iniquity on Jesus (v. 6), Paul said in 2 Corinthians 5 that God made Jesus who had no sin to be sin for us (v. 21). Peter said in 1 Peter 2 that Jesus bore our sins in his body on the tree (v. 24). Do you see it?

God, who is the victim of all sin, deems it acceptable for Jesus to become responsible for all our sin. Only God the victim of sin could make such a decision. And only Jesus could take such a responsibility because he alone of all men was sinless. So the sinless Jesus, the innocent Lamb of God, takes our sin. But where to?


Where he takes our sin

He takes it to the cross to face the judgement and wrath of God that it deserves. At Calvary the justice of God deals with our sin in the way that the law of God demands. The holy wrath of God falls upon our sin, but that sin is now upon Jesus.

Jesus the Lamb of God dies in our place. He is forsaken by his Father. Justice is satisfied. Sin is punished and now from the cross radiates divine love and mercy. There is forgiveness for guilty sinners.

What a gospel!

# 15.

# Stop trying and start trusting

After one Sunday morning service, a lady came up to me with tears in her eyes. She had heard the sermon and wanted to talk about God and her soul. I asked her if she was a Christian, and she replied that for some time she had been trying to be a Christian. Gently I said to her that she needed to stop trying and to start trusting Christ to save her.

She was genuinely concerned about her spiritual condition but, like many in her position, she was making a serious mistake. Trying to be a Christian never works because the best we could achieve would not be enough. Trying might appear to some to be an admirable exercise, but it is an exercise in delusion and inevitable failure. We do not become Christians by trying, but by trusting in what the Lord Jesus Christ has done for us.

The first step to becoming a Christian is to realize that there is nothing we can do to achieve this aim by our own efforts. That may appear to some to be a recipe for despair, but in fact it is not. A person is never so near to knowing God as when he realizes that he is hopeless and has nothing to offer the Lord.

The great question the Bible is always seeking to answer is, 'How can a man or woman be right with God?' It asks the question because it accepts the fact that we are not right with God. Man is a sinner and God is holy. There is, therefore, a great barrier between them.

The Bible also teaches that the wages of sin is death, and this means an eternity in hell. So this gives the question a great urgency. It is of no mere academic interest, as our eternal destiny rests upon it.

## So what is the answer?

Basically there are two answers offered us — law or grace. Law includes just about every system of religion or morals that say you must do this or go there in order to be saved. It teaches that man's salvation is in his own hands. Grace says that man is helpless and can do nothing to save himself. Salvation, therefore, has to be all of God.

The two answers are irreconcilable. They have nothing in common, and both cannot be right. So which is correct?

Are you confused by the gospel? If so, it is because you are allowing man's theories to distract from the basically simple message of God.

*We are sinners.*

*We cannot save ourselves.*

*Jesus is the only Saviour*
*    and we need him alone to save us.*

*There is nothing confusing about that.*

*So believe it and act upon it.*

For Christmas I was given some water-colour paints. I had never painted before, but tried it anyway. I soon discovered that I had no artistic talent whatsoever, but I was enjoying it. My first efforts looked as if a five-year-old had done them. But I began to improve, and soon my paintings began to look as if a six-year-old had done them. Then I went to the library and borrowed a video on 'Water Colouring for Beginners'. As I watched the expert at work, it all looked so easy — it always does when you watch experts.

What does this have to do with salvation? We need to know that, in the matter of salvation, there are no experts. We are all children groping around, and all our efforts are weak and ineffective. But this is exactly how it should be. Jesus said, 'I tell you the truth, anyone who will not receive the kingdom of God like a little child will never enter it' (Mark 10:15).

We need to see that there is nothing we can do to save ourselves, but that Jesus has done all that is needed.

This brings us back to the question, 'How do we become Christians?'

It is by faith in Christ who loved us and died for us. It is by faith in what the grace of God has accomplished for us. Grace, all the time, points us to Christ. The apostle Paul never got over the amazing fact that Christ loved him. His whole past life had been dedicated to destroying the work of Christ, yet still Christ loved him. This had to be an act of grace because it certainly was not earned or deserved. Grace is always free and unmerited, and addresses itself to us as guilty sinners.

To say that God loves sinners is a tremendous thing, but it is not the whole gospel. The gospel is that Christ loved me and *gave himself for me*. The gospel erupts in its full majestic splendour at the cross. There is no gospel message that does not include the substitutionary, atoning death of Jesus. Christ giving himself for me refers to him dying instead of me, paying the price of my sin.

In and of itself, Christ loving sinners does not change anything. Sin still had to be dealt with. Love finds the only way of doing this, by Jesus dying in our place — Jesus bearing our sin, our curse, our judgement, and purchasing salvation for us.

There is nothing that you can do that can in any way match what Christ has done. So it is futile to try. Just come in faith to the Lord Jesus as a helpless sinner asking for mercy and forgiveness.

*This is enough. God says so.*

# 16.

# Saul of Tarsus

If pigs could fly. That's exactly how Ananias felt in Acts 9 when he heard that Saul of Tarsus had become a Christian.

He was not the only one who found this too impossible to believe. When the Christians in Jerusalem heard about it they reacted in the same way. To be fair to these folk their doubts were reasonable. Saul was the great persecutor, the great enemy of the church (Acts 9:1-2). But it was not impossible because salvation is all of grace.

Grace makes the impossible possible. There are no more thrilling words in the Bible than those of Jesus in Mark 10:27: 'With man this is impossible, but not with God; all things are possible with God.'

## The old Saul

Before Saul became a Christian he was deeply religious. He tells us in Philippians 3:5-6: 'circumcised on the eighth day, of the people of Israel, of the tribe of Benjamin, a Hebrew of Hebrews; in regard to the law, a Pharisee; as for zeal, persecuting the church; as for legalistic righteousness, faultless'. His religious pedigree was impeccable, but this was the problem. Religion gets in the way of true faith, because religion gives a man very preconceived views of God. But more than that, religion centres on man, not God, and certainly not on Jesus.

Religion views things horizontally not vertically. It measures thing by man's standards not God's. Religion always minimizes sin and God's demands. You can see how Saul did this in Philippians 3:6:'as for legalistic righteousness, faultless'. Saul was convinced he had not broken the law of God. It was exactly same with the rich young ruler in Mark 10:17-20. When confronted by Jesus with the law of God he said, 'all these I have kept since I was a boy'.

It is always the same. Religion gives an exalted view of self and an inferior view of God. We can test this by our commonly held beliefs:

- Try your best because that is all God expects;
- As long as good deeds outweigh bad it's ok;
- There is no such place as hell.

Such an attitude has to change if a person is to become a Christian; but how can this change? Only God can do it. So it is fortunate for us that all things are possible with God.

## Making the impossible possible

Consider for a moment what salvation does. It takes a person who is dead in sin and makes him spiritually alive. It deals once and for all with that person's sin. It deals, to God's satisfaction — and this is crucial — with God's holy anger on that sin. It meets all of God's requirements: the sin is punished, the law of God is honoured not ignored. Jesus taking responsibility for our sin achieves all this. The Saviour takes our guilt and punishment and dies in our place. It is totally impossible for man to do any of this. By the biblical definition, salvation has to be of God.

So how does God do the impossible and save the sinner, whether it is a man desperately opposed to Christ, or a totally irreligious atheist, or a nice respectable pillar of society?

There is only one way that God saves and it is through Jesus. God may use many different methods to bring the sinner to Jesus but that is where all sinners must come if they are to know the full and free salvation that God provides.

First of all, God has to make the sinner aware of the reality of his own sin. Salvation is from the guilt and consequence of sin. If I don't see the terrifying position my sin has put me in, if I cannot see I am facing judgement and hell, I will never see my need of the Saviour.

We can see Jesus doing this with the rich young ruler in Mark 10. The man seems to be a great prospect for salvation.

He comes seeking Christ, his attitude is humble as he falls on his knees, and he asks the right question about eternal life. If this had taken place today in some evangelistic crusade we would have had him sign a decision card, pronto!

But how does Jesus deal with him? Jesus takes him to the law of God (v. 19). Some might be amazed at this and say, 'Jesus, don't you know how to lead a soul to Christ? It's not law but love that he needs to hear of.' Why did Jesus do this? The answer is in the man's reply in verse 20. The man has no awareness of his own personal sin and guilt. And you cannot be saved without this. No matter what else he does right, if there is no conviction of sin, there can be no repentance, and if there is no repentance there can be no salvation. Who says so? Jesus does: 'Unless you repent, you too will all perish' (Luke 13:3).

As we have seen, Saul was exactly the same as the rich young ruler. He believed that as far as God's law was concerned, he was faultless. That allusion was shattered on the road to Damascus when he met Jesus. 'Why do you persecute me?' Jesus asked him. Persecuting the Christ, the Messiah: could there be a greater sin? He may not have been aware of what he was doing, but still this is God's accusation against him.

Has God been doing this to you? Has he been showing you your sin? Are you beginning to think differently about your sin? Previously you dismissed sin with, 'Well, everyone does it, so it does not matter'. But you cannot do that now.

It disturbs you; it makes you feel guilty. That is God at work in your heart and conscience.

It is impossible for you to deal with your sin. It is possible for you to turn over a new leaf and change your lifestyle, to put right certain things in your life. You can do all that, but you cannot change your nature. The Bible asks, 'Can … the leopard [change] its spots?' (Jeremiah 13:23). No. It is impossible; and so also is it impossible for a sinner to make himself acceptable to God.

If this is to happen, God must do it. Only God can make the impossible possible. *The gospel is the account of how God does this.*

Because God is holy, sin is an immense problem. He cannot tolerate it and will not have it in his presence. And he will never make allowances for sin or excuse it. So what can be done about this problem? God deals with it himself by sending Jesus into the world to be our sinbearer, our substitute, to take responsibility for our sin and guilt, and to take the punishment that sin deserved. That is what happened on the cross.

| Listen to Peter: | '[Jesus] bore our sins in his body on the cross' (1 Peter 2:24). |
| Listen to Paul: | 'God made him who had no sin to be sin for us' (2 Corinthians 5:21). |
| Listen to Jesus: | 'The Son of Man [came] to give his life as a ransom for many' (Matthew 20:28; Mark 10:45). |

## What does this accomplish?

- It means that the immense problem of my sin has been dealt with to God's satisfaction;
- It means that God's law has been fully satisfied;
- It means that God is now able to forgive all my sin in a way that is perfectly just. He has not turned a blind eye to sin but dealt with it, punished it, and removed it from my account for ever.

These are the facts of the gospel. Now listen to the invitation of the gospel. 'Come to me,' says Jesus in Matthew 11:28. But there is still a problem. Sin holds us back. Jesus said in John 5:40: 'You refuse to come to me to have life.'

But the rich young ruler *did* come to Jesus. He came humbly. He came seeking eternal life. True. But he did not come in repentance. He could not do that because he had no conviction of sin. So does this cancel out all that Jesus has done on the cross? NO. When God planned our salvation he knew of the awful hold that sin has on us, so he provided the answer. And yet again we see the impossible being achieved. Yet again we are faced with the fact that salvation has to be all of grace.

Listen to Jesus facing the problem. John 6:44: 'No one can come to me.' What a terrible prospect. But Jesus does not finish there. He goes on to say, 'unless the Father who sent me draws him'.

Do you see what Jesus is saying? Not only does God have to provide the means of salvation, he also has to provide the method. The only way for a sinner to be saved is for God the Father to love him, Jesus to die for him, and the Holy Spirit to draw him to God.

## How does the Holy Spirit draw us to God?

The Holy Spirit draws us to God *through the message of the gospel*. The preaching of the gospel creates conviction of sin. But there is more. The Holy Spirit also gives the faith and repentance that enables us to receive the gift of salvation.

If you now know the reality of your sin; if you long to be acceptable to God and want this more than anything else; if you believe that what Jesus did is enough to deal with your sin; then that is the work of the Holy Spirit. He is drawing you, so come trusting Jesus alone to save you. Come and ask for pardon and forgiveness.

Faith is to take what grace offers. It does not add to what grace has done. It grabs gratefully.

# 17.
# Electronic ticketing

I received an invitation to preach in California. As the time drew near for my departure I grew somewhat concerned because I had not received a ticket from the churches who had invited me to preach. But they were soon on the telephone telling me not to worry because I did not need a ticket. However, this did not relieve my concern; rather, it deepened it. Of course I needed a ticket. Everyone knows you cannot fly without a ticket. What on earth were those folk in California talking about?

They then started to explain to me something called electronic ticketing. Apparently all I had to do was to present myself at the airlines desk at Heathrow Airport, tell them who I was, show them my passport and they would then give me a ticket.

I had never heard of this before and I was rather dubious. I wanted the comfort of a ticket in my hand before I left home. They again had to reassure me that it would be all right. 'It has all been taken care of at this end,' they said.

Of course, all my fears were unfounded. It had indeed all been taken care of at the other end; the folk inviting me knew it, and the airline knew it, even if I was a bit uncertain.

*The grace of God is something like that* — it has all been taken care of at the other end.

One day I will set out on the most important journey anyone can take — from this life to the next. I will have to stand before God and he will say, 'Who are you?'

I will answer by giving him my name. 'O, yes,' God will reply, 'you are the one my Son died for and paid the debt for your sins; you are the one Jesus loved and saved. Come on into heaven, you are welcome because of what Jesus has done for you.'

Salvation is all taken care of by Jesus the Saviour. This is a great comfort to a sinner like myself who is always full of doubts and uncertainties. Has Jesus taken care of your salvation?

When God planned the salvation of sinners he did it in such a way as to take into account our doubts and fears. Electronic ticketing was new to me, and this was why I was uncertain, but it did mean that I could never lose my ticket. All I had to do was to turn up and it was waiting for me. Salvation by grace means that we can never lose our salvation. Because it has all been taken care of at the other end, and because Jesus has done it all, there is no possibility of us ever losing it.

All this is offered us in the gospel. The guarantee Jesus gives in the gospel is:

'Trust in God; trust also in me. In my Father's house are many rooms; if it were not so, I would have told you. I am going there to prepare a place for you. And if I go and prepare a place for you, I will come back and take you to be with me that you also may be where I am'

(John 14:1-3).

# 18.

# The jailor at Philippi

The story in Acts 16 of the jailor at Philippi is one of great significance. Here was a man not interested in God and certainly with no intention of meeting God. Religion, let alone Christianity, could not have been further away from his thinking. Yet through a series of remarkable circumstances he is led to ask: 'What must I do to be saved?' Why he asked this question and what led up to it is a glorious illustration of the grace of God.

## Grace

Grace exists and is necessary for two reasons: the character of man and the character of God. Though man was created in the image of God, able to know and enjoy him, when man sinned he became separated from God, and sin has since dominated all his actions. He is now an alien to God his Maker, and because of his sinful character he can do nothing about it. God's character, on the other hand, is such that he cannot condone or overlook sin. His holiness, truth and justice demand that man must be dealt with as he is, and that sin must be punished.

These two factors, taken on their own, would condemn all men to an eternity in hell. But God's character is also such that though he hates sin, yet he loves the guilty sinner who deserves his judgement. Divine love therefore plans salvation, and divine grace provides salvation. Grace is necessary, because without it sinful man has no hope; and grace is possible because of the loving and merciful character of God. Once this truth is grasped and understood, grace becomes the most thrilling thing there is.

Grace and salvation belong together as cause and effect (Ephesians 2:5; Titus 2:11). Grace is the cause of salvation. The gospel centres upon the great doctrine of justification by faith: it is in justification that we receive pardon for sin and peace with God, and justification is the product of divine grace (Romans 3:24). Grace flows from the tender heart of God the Father, and it is embodied in Jesus Christ the Son of God. It is Jesus who makes grace a reality by fulfilling the dictates of grace: he dies, the just for the unjust; he appeases the holy wrath of God; he sheds his blood to cover our sin, and he takes our sin away. All this is because of grace.

Very few people are converted the first time they hear the gospel; but grace will not take no for an answer and begins to work on the sinner's mind and conscience. Irresistible grace does not mean that God saves a man against his will; rather, grace seeks to change the will, until the sinner wants salvation more than anything else. Grace is not a way of helping sinners to be saved; it is God's way of salvation. In other words, grace is not given to aid or assist us; it is the power of God to save us.

## God at work

God brought this very ungodly jailor into contact with two Christians. Paul and Silas were in prison quite unjustly but also very much in the plan and will of God. If the jailor is to be saved he must hear the gospel so God brought the preachers into his jail. Then an earthquake wrecked the prison and the jailor in terror cries out: 'What must I do to be saved?' Probably at that moment he was not thinking of salvation from sin, but that was soon to change.

We can see the overriding hand of God in all these happenings, and the same is true to some degree or other in the salvation of every sinner. The initiative is always God's. Stop and examine your own life at this point. What has been happening to you over the past months and years? Almost certainly nothing as dramatic as an earthquake, but still here you are reading a Christian book. Would you have done that a year ago?

In your home, family or job, are events and circumstances causing you to think seriously about God for the first time? Perhaps the sudden death of a friend has hit you hard and you are thinking that it could have been you. Or it may be that all the terrible events which are happening in the world are causing you to think seriously about life and death.

Have you thought that this may be God speaking to you? Don't dismiss this as absurd. God dealt with the jailor in this way and with countless others since. He does it because he loves you and wants to save you.

## The question

The question was asked because of God's dealing with this man. He began to see his need and though at this point he may not have realized the full significance of the question, he was moving towards God.

We too should be asking what we must do to be saved. We have seen already in this book that we are all sinners. It does not matter what the sin is — murder, adultery, pride or gossip, all sin puts us under the wrath of God. This is why we need saving from the consequence of our sin, which is judgement and hell.

## The answer

Paul explained the full gospel to the jailor and provides for him the answer to his question: 'Believe in the Lord Jesus, and you will be saved.'

Belief in the Bible is not just an intellectual response of the mind. The heart too must be involved. In Romans 10:10 Paul says, 'For it is with your heart that you believe and are justified.' Believing in the mind, that is, accepting the truth concerning the facts of the gospel, is crucial; but it is not enough. James said even the devils believe in this way (James 2:19). In Romans 10, Paul is not talking of a superficial confession accompanied by no more than a token faith. Belief in the heart refers to a faith that takes hold of the whole inner man.

*Intellect*: This means we believe the facts. We believe Jesus was born of the Virgin. We believe in his deity and sinlessness. We believe he died for sinners and that God raised him from the dead.

*Emotions*: Our belief is not a cold, matter-of-fact belief, but it moves us. True belief will both thrill and frighten. We are thrilled to think God loves us and frightened to think of the consequence of not having Jesus as our Saviour.

*Will*: You act upon what you believe. Your belief causes you to flee in faith and repentance to Jesus. All this is included in what it means to believe in Jesus. To believe means to have faith in Jesus. There is an old Sunday school acrostic that explains what faith means:

**f**orsaking **all i t**ake **h**im.

If you believe intellectually and your emotions are stirred by the gospel then turn now to Jesus for forgiveness of sin. You are being drawn by God, so come to Jesus and come with his own guarantee: 'whoever comes to me I will never drive away' (John 6:37).

# 19.

# The last train

I stood on the platform of life, as the last train for heaven was about to board its passengers. The platform was filled with happy, smiling people anticipating their journey.

I was rather apprehensive about boarding, wondering if there would be room for me. The station master, seeing my hesitation, said, 'Come along, sir, I will take you to your seat.' He led me to a seat especially reserved for me with my name on it. He smiled at my surprise, and said, 'All seats are reserved on this train.'

I settled into my seat and dozed off as the journey started. I was awakened when the train went through the *Tunnel of Pride*. A fear took hold of me. Would the finger of pride point me out as one of its regular customers? There had been so much pride in my life that I felt sure it would accuse me. The conductor could see I was disturbed and reassured me that no one was ever put off the train for heaven. When I confided in him about my fear, he said, 'No one is on this train because he deserves it. You are here, not because of righteous things you have done, but because of

God's mercy.' I knew this, but I needed to be reminded of it often.

Soon, we were out of the tunnel and travelling through a flat plain. The fields looked lovely, but they were spiritually ugly. Fields of lust, lies and jealousy once again served to remind me of my sin. How could I be on the way to heaven with such terrible things in my life? The conductor once again came to my help by reminding me that the blood of Jesus cleanses from all sin.

Why did I forget so essential a truth? My peace returned as I began to think of the amazing grace of God that had saved me. I talked to the other passengers and we soon discovered that none of us had bought a ticket for the journey. All the costs had been met by the Lord Jesus Christ. Together we began to praise him for such love and mercy. As we did, doubts and uncertainties vanished. Our trust and confidence were strengthened in what Jesus had done for us.

Meanwhile, back on the platform, another group of people was gathering. One man seemed to epitomize them all. He took an enormous amount of baggage with him. Surrounding him were dozens of cases filled with his sin. 'Is that all mine?' he asked. He was told yes, and there was even more. Two trucks of cases and trunks then arrived. The stench of the sin contained in them even sickened their owner.

One case in particular had a foul smell. It was labelled 'unbelief'. The man looked at it and wept. He remembered all the occasions when the way to heaven had been shown him. His thoughts went back to the many times when the gospel of Jesus was told him, but he had rejected it with arrogant unbelief.

*He believed now, but it was too late. The last train for heaven had gone and he was left with his sin and the next train for hell.*

The above story is only a parable, but it reflects the truth for every one of us. Which train are you going on?

If you were honest with yourself, you would admit that you are not as good as you would like to be. If that is true by your standards, what do you think you are by God's standards?

By God's standards…

- We are all sinners;
- He does not call us his children but his enemies;
- This sin puts us under his judgement.

Like the man with the baggage, you have missed the train to heaven. The situation of the sinner before the holy God is hopeless, and it would remain so apart from the grace of God.

God's answer to our sin is Jesus. He alone is the Saviour who can take our sin away and purchase for us a full forgiveness and salvation. You need Jesus and you need him today. The matter is urgent, so pray to him for pardon and ask for mercy.

The last train for heaven has not yet departed, and there is room on it for you if you know the Lord Jesus Christ as your Saviour. Get your seat reserved now.

A wide range of Christian books is available from Evangelical Press. If you would like a free catalogue please write to us or contact us by e-mail. Alternatively, you can view the whole catalogue online at our web site:

www.evangelicalpress.org.

Evangelical Press
Faverdale North, Darlington, DL3 0PH, England

e-mail: sales@evangelicalpress.org

Evangelical Press USA
P. O. Box 825, Webster, New York 14580, USA

e-mail: usa.sales@evangelicalpress.org